SPANISH WRITERS
of 1936

SPANISH WRITERS
of 1936

*Crisis and Commitment in the Poetry of
the Thirties and Forties*

AN ANTHOLOGY OF LITERARY STUDIES AND ESSAYS

———

*Edited by Jaime Ferrán
and Daniel P. Testa*

TAMESIS BOOKS LIMITED

LONDON

Colección Támesis

SERIE A — MONOGRAFIAS XXXI

Copyright. All rights reserved.
London, 1973

ISBN 0 900411 71 6

Designed and Printed in England
at the Compton Press for
TAMESIS BOOKS LIMITED
LONDON

Contents

Preface

This collection of studies stems in part from a symposium which was convened during November, 1967 by the present editors under the auspices of the Centro de Estudios Hispánicos and the Department of Romance Languages of Syracuse University. Some twenty Spanish writers and American Hispanists assembled on the Syracuse University campus for an unprecedented public discussion of literary matters long considered to be sensitive and polemical. The bulk of those proceedings, entirely in Spanish, was published in a recent number of Symposium *(Summer,* 1968*).* From that issue, several articles have been taken and presented in this volume in English translation. Many of the remaining essays included here are being published for the first time.

Acknowledgements

The two articles by José Luis Aranguren, the two articles by Manuel Durán and the articles by José Ferrater-Mora, Ildefonso-Manuel Gil and José María Valverde first appeared in *Symposium*, vol. XXIX, no. 2 (Summer, 1968), and are here reproduced in translation by kind permission of the Syracuse University Press.

Poems XVII, XVIII and XX from W. H. Auden's *Look, Stranger*! are quoted in Manuel Durán's article "Miguel Hernández, poet of clay and of light", by kind permission of Faber and Faber Ltd.

The preparation and publication costs of this volume were met in part by the kind support of Frank Piskor, former Vice-Chancellor for Academic Affairs, and Newell W. Rossman Jr., Vice-Chancellor for University Relations, Syracuse University.

General Introduction

The articles gathered in this volume represent viewpoints and studies on the literary ambiance of a relatively brief but turbulent period of Spanish history. The year 1936, which marked the beginning of a tragic war between irreconcilable ideologies, is one of the important turning-points in contemporary Spanish life. The repercussions of the Spanish Civil War (1936–39) resounded across national frontiers with compelling foreboding that announced the demise of a fledgling parliamentary democracy. Because of the War's impact on national and international affairs, its political and military aspects have long dominated in popular and scholarly writings, and it is these aspects which by and large have overshadowed the understanding and evaluation of the literature of those years.

The outbreak of the Civil War, with all its subsequent individual and collective horrors, seared the lives of Spanish writers both young and old, but particularly of those who came of literary age a few years before or after the actual event. Thus, the historical basis for the term "Generation of 1936". But in applying this kind of chronological label, we should be careful not to insist on time limits that are overly rigid or specific, for no matter how abruptly a cultural upheaval may seem to occur, the truth of the matter is that such upheavals will inevitably have traceable antecedents in the years immediately before and visible consequences after.

Many of the perspectives offered in this volume, therefore, focus quite properly on events and trends that date from the early thirties to the forties and fifties. There is abundant evidence that many writers of the early thirties were already evolving in directions that only later became manifest in the events themselves. As is well known, the blood shed in the Civil War was tragically great, the brutalization extreme. The anguish for most Spanish authors did not end, however, with the termination of hostilities. Among the exiled writers, a few immediately found the freedom and distance to put their war experiences and observations into essay or fictional form. In the exhausted and regimented homeland, an ever-increasing number of voices in the early and middle forties began to find authentic expression for the harsh realities gnawing unspeakably at the innermost soul.

In casting a glance back to the two or three decades in question, we can readily agree with those critics who see the Spanish Civil War as a gulf between two very different worlds. Spanish literature is dominated from the First World War to the early 30s by the avant-garde. After 1940, the dominant trend is towards a simplified and more direct expression of experience.[1] But a true perspective of pre-Civil War literature does not rightly begin with the vanguard writers, whose original, and sometimes strident, innovations became the dominant esthetic for well over a decade. They form only one constellation – an impressive one, to be sure – in the brilliant galaxy of intellectuals and writers who emerged on the horizon at the beginning of the present century. The defeat suffered by colonial Spain in the Spanish-American War in 1898 was the catalyst that aroused, through writers like Ganivet, Unamuno, Baroja, Azorín, and others, a nation in which a lethargic intellectual and political life had settled over its people.

Along with the political, moral, and spiritual preoccupations polemically and ardently pursued by many of the 1898 writers, a parallel reform in literature began to flourish after Rubén Darío, its principal progenitor, came to Spain in the late 19th century. This movement, known as Modernism in Hispanic letters, represented a blend of *fin de siècle* estheticism and some features of European symbolist poetry. In Spain, Modernism's most fervent follower was perhaps Juan Ramón Jiménez, from whose poetry stem the following trends present in the verse of the 1920s: neopopularism, a marked reliance on the senses, the need to evade everyday reality, and the writer's total dedication in the pursuit of beauty.

Spanish poetry after World War I is further complicated by the specific avant-garde developments, such as "Ultraísmo" and "Creacionismo", as well as the Spanish counterpart to French Surrealism. But transcending these significant though often short-lived movements are the individual achievements of a group of poets in the ascendancy after 1920, who have been called the Generation of 1927 by critics who saw in the 300th anniversary of Góngora's death a basis for generational identity. In drawing upon the highly visual and sensorial aspects of Baroque poetry, especially the techniques of style found in Góngora's major poems, poets like García Lorca, Alberti, Gerardo Diego, Jorge Guillén, Luis Cernuda, etc., produced works in which virtuosity and craftsmanship were given primacy over sentiment and ideological content. After serving as a central force for a few years, neo-Baroque poetics began to be replaced by a search for a more simple, less ornate statement. A new movement, called "Garcilasism" (after the Spanish Renaissance poet of melancholy, Garcilaso), was born in the works of Germán Bléiberg (*Sonetos amorosos*, 1936), Luis Rosales (*Abril*, 1935), and Miguel Hernández (*El rayo que no cesa*, 1936). The evolution of Spanish poetry during the thirties can best be exemplified with the work of this last named writer, whose first book (*Perito en lunas*, 1930) was written in the wake of the neo-Baroque revival, in contrast to the changes seen in his second book of poems, *El rayo que no cesa*. In addition, Hernández' poetry, by 1936, is definitively visited by a conscience of protest and rebellion that arises directly out of his

---

[1]As Manuel Durán puts it, " . . . the prewar styles were too subjective, too refined, too subtle to stand the test of conflict, war, collective emotions. They had to be discarded during the war and were to be replaced by simpler styles, more in keeping with the collective mood of war and the collective angers and frustrations of the post-war world. This applies not only to lyrical poetry, but also to the novel and drama". "Spanish Literature Since the War" in *On Contemporary Literature* (ed. R. Kostelanetz; New York, 1964), pp. 194–95.

relationship with Pablo Neruda and other writers who had become acutely aware of the need for a rhetoric of violence. The two dominant characteristics of the first wave of the Generation of 1936 are therefore "Garcilasism" and protest; the latter characteristic will grow in importance for the second wave of writers of this Generation, who make their appearance in the immediate post-war period (Gabriel Celaya, Angela Figuera, Victoriano Crémer, among others).

We should also note here another literary event that merits attention : the publication in 1944 of *Hijos de la ira,* which, like other post-Civil War developments, emerges from the ruins and spiritual malaise of Spanish life. Its author, Dámaso Alonso – distinguished as a professor and literary critic – belongs chronologically to the previous generation, but with this collection of poems, he places himself squarely in the midst of younger writers. An influential book, *Hijos de la ira* is characterized by its forceful content of protest and questioning and by a sense of anguish and dread that magnifies and distorts everyday fears into undefinable terrors.[2]

In looking at the decade of the thirties, admittedly a complex historical period, two significant facts stand out : the fundamental changes in literary currents that were occurring in Europe as well as in Spain; and the total upheaval caused by a civil war in Spain which was to affect all aspects of life. This collection of essays attempts to focus most specifically and most validly on the literary consequences brought about by those two historical facts. The ultimate value of the analyses lies in our ability to comprehend the significance of the literary experiences offered by a group of writers who were the actual participants and witnesses of that embittered and chaotic time. By increasing our own knowledge and sensitivity to the crises suffered by that Generation, the turmoil of our present day will perhaps seem less strange and less frightening.

[2]The historical significance of *Hijos de la ira* – as well as its aesthetic values and meaning – was consistently reaffirmed in April, 1969, during a symposium that was convened on the Syracuse University campus by the present editors to celebrate the 25th anniversary of that work's appearance.

I
HISTORY OF THE TERM "GENERATION OF *1936*"

Introduction

The term "Generation of 1936" has been involved in controversy ever since it was created and proposed by Homero Serís in a brief article published in *Books Abroad*, XIX (1945), 336-40, and in a slightly revised Spanish version, "La generación española de 1936", issued in pamphlet form by Syracuse University, Syracuse, New York, 1946. It was Serís' conviction that the Spanish Civil War was the principal factor in the formation of this new literary grouping: "Just as a war was the cause and the immediate occasion of the crystallization in Spain of the so-called Generation of 1898, just so another war brought into being a new literary generation which I should like to call the Generation of 1936." The outline presented by Serís was a schematic attempt to draw upon Julius Petersen's categories as applied by Pedro Salinas to the Generation of 1898. Critical reaction to Serís was in the main favourable, although an important Spanish critic, Guillermo de Torre, questioned the validity of Serís' formulation – recognizing nonetheless the latter's provocative and boldly speculative manner of viewing history – in an article entitled "La supuesta generación española de 1936", *Cabalgata* (Buenos Aires, October 1, 1945). Some years later, another Spanish critic, Ricardo Gullón – a member himself of this would-be generation – established a more systematic survey of the writers of the Generation of 1936, focussing on the most crucial problems dealing with what he called the "splintered generation". Gullón's study, which appeared in *Asomante*, XV (1959), evoked additional comment from Guillermo de Torre, who confirmed his original objections to the existence of that generation. Torre's second article and a revision of Gullón's study were both published in the double issue of *Insula* (no. 224-225, 1965), which solicited a wide cross-section of opinion relating to the Generation of 1936. Since these two writers represent broad and contrasting viewpoints, we offer their essays here – in English translation – as useful background material for our readers.

The Generation of 1936*

RICARDO GULLON

On several occasions I have stated precisely how careful one should be in handling the concept of a literary generation. Such a concept is not a key to solving problems of literary historiography, but a rather crude instrument for fixing positions and establishing relationships among the writers of a particular period. Without losing sight of this limitation, I have decided to speak about a Spanish Generation of 1936, named after the cruel and heartbreaking event of our Civil War, which not only named the generation, but branded it; some of its men died in it, others suffered imprisonment, not a few lived or are living in exile.

Can one speak, even with all sorts of qualifications, of a generation of '36? If we undertook the analysis of conditions stipulated by Petersen and understood them rigidly, the answer would not be affirmative, but it would not be difficult to narrow down the concept by basing it on other assumptions and even accepting, though with necessary flexibility, those of the German professor. A point of departure for the study could be the relative unity with which the group of writers born between 1906 and 1914 appears in Spanish letters, that is, those who were born in the years prior to the first World War and whose fate it was to suffer the Spanish Civil War. Beneath the evident differences, the unconcealable disparities, and the fact of having taken part in the conflict from opposite sides, the people of '36 have much in common, and they resemble each other more than they could resemble the members of previous groups or generations, although they may be related, or have similarities, to them. The generational and paradoxically unifying event was the Civil War, which lasted from July, 1936 to April, 1939. This dreadful event marked the members of this generation, for they suffered it directly and at close range.

Very different from the people who, more advanced in age and scepticism, kept themselves at a prudent distance from the events of the War, the younger people lived close to these events and some participated in them. As a consequence of the dispersal begun by the War itself, the generation may seem divided into two camps. This is an optical illusion, and, in reality, if separation exists with respect to distance, it does not emerge, except in a few cases, with respect to attitudes.

*From Ricardo Gullón, *La invención del 98 y otros ensayos* (Madrid, 1968); the translation is by Francis L. Trice, with revisions under the author's supervision.

This generation's destiny was difficult to bear, but it is not fair to charge these writers with blame that is not personally theirs and to hold them accountable for the destruction of the inner unity of their generation, for the dispersion and the disaster. Perhaps as a "generation" it has been liquidated; probably the future will offer no opportunity for effective political action or for real influence over the country, but it is better to abstain from any prediction in this respect, since it would be reckless, to say the least.

Let us see what might be the weaknesses of this group of writers and let us note, objectively, their accomplishments.

It is true that the majority of its members found themselves at some point out of touch with the people. But this reproach is too vague; it could be applied equally to "the generation" of 1925. If one means by this distance from the working class and its problems, then one must recognize the reality of that separation. The problems were treated at the intellectual and spiritual levels, at a relative distance from everyday reality, and this carried the majority to a kind of sentimental idealism, which left the physical aspects of the nation untouched and which had little hope for success.

There were among these men some pure idealists, a characteristic truer of them in the year 1936 than at the present time. It was perhaps inevitable that a few of them were led into cynicism or into opportunism by way of scepticism, but in general they have remained true to themselves.

Political apathy — scepticism — is today one of their predominant traits. Is it fair to reproach them for that? After the difficult experience of the war, it is not strange that a mood of tiredness, aversion and disgust toward politics and things political should overcome the best of them, and incline them toward the sceptical attitude of persons who have come back after receiving a harsh and unforgettable lesson.

But they were not always that way. In their youth they were enthusiastic and hopeful; they believed that Spain could be rebuilt by peace and work, and they fought for this ideal. But the Civil War brutally dashed their hopes, leading them into indifference in which they lived, aimless and disheartened. As a consequence of this indifference the generation has become overly prudent, and its prudence is revealed in a very praiseworthy characteristic : the desire for conciliation among Spaniards. In this case, conciliation naturally implies reconciliation and cessation of the state of conflict that still exists in Spain.

The most laudable feature of this generation, I believe, has been the decision to reject the division of Spaniards into "the conquerors and the conquered", a division deliberately set forth by elements of both sides. This division is anachronistic and absurd, but when, against all reason and wisdom, an attempt was made to establish it at the end of the Civil War, it was no less absurd and its effects were more cruel.

The generation withstood the test of the War, but in peace it retreated to selfish positions. I do not know if it was caution so much as punishment and fear of finding itself alone; its members easily forgot their duty to lead and their obligation to be witnesses. The intellectual is, or should be, the conscience of his people, and a conscience has to be critical, not complacent.

Our generation has been too serious, in its life and in its work. At first, it was not; it was vital, jubilant, anxious to participate and communicate. To reproach it for its present lack of gaiety is to forget the erosion of the years and to disregard the conditions of the world in which it has been our lot to live. If we look beyond Spain's borders, if we look at the contemporary generations of Europe and the New World, we find them less capable of gaiety and no more confident in the future. Our excessive seriousness and prudence is in direct relation to the problems by which we feel challenged and to our real or presumed incapacity to solve, or attempt to solve, them.

The youthful years of this generation were spent in the War, and upon reaching maturity it felt that it had been deprived of its best years. Perhaps the same thing always occurs, but the men of '36 have the sensation that through some incredible game of destiny their youth was whisked away when they were living it most enthusiastically. Too naively, they wonder why such a joke was played on them. Prudence, caution, fondness for exactitude and precision, give everyone his due, do no harm to anyone . . . and, meanwhile, noiselessly, with stealthy steps, youth was irredeemably escaping. Yes; it is an old story.

The generation of 1936 is, by and large, made up of decent people. It is not known whether they have committed vile acts, or even any of those amusingly mischievous acts that were a hallmark of writers long ago. They were not responsible for condemning or rejecting previous movements, or for virulent attacks, unfair reactions to anyone. They have observed life around them with love, and, in a few cases, with faith. As opposed to the religious indifference of preceding generations, some of its members are believers and Catholics.

The generation of 1936 cannot be considered either "right-wing" or "left-wing" according to the classifications so long in vogue. It is a moderate generation, tolerant and comprehensive, opposed to worn-out conventions and factions. One could not say of it, in all fairness, that it has contributed to widening the existing division between Spaniards. Believers or unbelievers, they are fighting, with rare exceptions, for harmony and tolerance. They are not the ones, I believe, to light bonfires in which to burn the works of their enemy and much less the enemy himself.

They are patriots, like the "Modernists" and the "Postmodernists" and they love Spain, from near or from afar, with a passion for justice that saves them from conformity. No, they are not conformists, since conformity is submission to ideas, norms, and conditions of life and thought inherited from a tradition that wishes to maintain itself without being subjected to discussion and analysis.

As far as literature is concerned, whilst not accepting all the attitudes (and even less the formulas) of preceding writers, they are not revolutionaries, nor innovators, in the way that the avant-garde writers were. Toward 1935 the "isms" were losing strength. An entire period of experimentation and adventure was temporarily over, awaiting the time when it might start again, giving way to new impulses and different oscillations of the pendulum.

Having reached this point, I think it would be useful to indicate the names of those who, in my judgment, figure in the generation of 1936. I do not begin without having thought about the most satisfactory criterion for composing a list of names of those who constitute the generation, and of course the list is open to eventual correction. After some hesitation I chose to accept a somewhat ambiguous, but sufficiently clear norm that simultaneously takes into account age, dedication to literature at the time indicated for defining the generation (1936), companionship, publication in the same reviews, literary collections, newspapers and other publications, and participation in the experiences of the period from the same centers of activity.

The poets of the generation, according to this norm, would be: Miguel Hernández, Luis Rosales, Leopoldo and Juan Panero, Luis Felipe Vivanco, Ildefonso-Manuel Gil, Germán Bleiberg, José Antonio Muñoz Rojas, José María Luelmo, Pedro Pérez Clotet, Rafael Duyos, Gabriel Celaya, Arturo Serrano Plaja and Juan Gil Albert. In the group of prose writers would be: Enrique Azcoaga, José Antonio Maravall, Antonio Sánchez Barbudo, Ramón Faraldo, Eusebio García Luengo, María Zambrano, José Ferrater Mora and myself.

To this central nucleus of the generation must be added the names of those who joined it during the Civil War or immediately thereafter, and who earlier, it may be said, were linked by ideas to those mentioned above: Dionisio Ridruejo, José Luis Cano, Ramón de Garcíasol, Pedro Laín Entralgo, Juan López Morillas, José Luis Aranguren, Francisco Ynduráin, Julián Marías, Segundo Serrano Poncela, José Antonio Gaya Nuño, José Suárez Carreño, Jorge Campos, Ernesto G. Da Cal and José Manuel Blecua. There are writers of later affiliation, but whose inclusion among the latter would not be excessive, for example: Concha Zardoya, Juan Ruiz Peña, Luis Monguió, Carlos Clavería and Antonio Rodríguez Huéscar.

I realize that there are names missing. Some are of people who strayed from literature into politics, the theatre, journalism or other more or less substantial substitutes. Time will tell who, among those mentioned, constitute the group that is to endure, and the reader will forgive me for not assuming the risky role of prophet. If I have omitted someone of importance, it is due to forgetfulness and not to prejudice.

As the prudent reader will note, I have tried to compose this account in the most complete, comprehensive, and objective manner possible. A brief review of the names quoted will show that the generation of '36 is made up of important writers, some of them with valuable works. Among the poets there are two or three who can be favorably compared with those of the generation of 1925. Among the prose writers there likewise can be found names of the first order. It would be worthwhile to compile a bibliography of the writings of these men to show, without further discussion, the quality of their contributions to Hispanic letters.

I cannot speak of the origins of this generation without taking into account personal memories. It is inevitable: this generation is mine; I know or am acquainted with all its members; some are close friends with whom I shared hours of happiness and times of sorrow. Furthermore, I do not believe that the intrusion of a personal element will mar the account in this case. Just the opposite: it may perhaps give a documentary interest to the exposition and make it more vivid.

The generation of '36 did not emerge fully armed. To parody a well-known quotation, I shall say that "it began by not existing". Isolated youths timidly entered the fray in different places. Timidly, I say, even though this timidity sometimes might have seemed like boldness. In my province, León, as far back as 1928, Juan and Leopoldo Panero, Luis Alonso Luengo and I, with other friends later lost to literature (one of them was killed in the war), published a little adolescent magazine called *Humo,* which was perhaps the first review published by one of the groups that would make up the new movement. (Gerardo Diego later called this group the Astorga School.)

Something on the same lines occurred a short time later in several cities, and before 1930 the most restless youths were agitating in Madrid, impatient to express their innermost thoughts and feelings. New relationships, new friendships were formed and were based on impulses and sympathies that were deeper than those of regional identification. The University, the "Ateneo", the Academy of Jurisprudence, the coffee-houses, and in some cases the editorial offices of newspapers and magazines were the gathering places.

The struggle against the Dictatorship of Primo de Rivera, and at a later date the agitation against the government of General Berenguer; the activities of the Federación Universitaria Española; the exile of Unamuno; the resignations of Professors Jiménez Asúa, Ortega, de los Ríos, Sánchez Román and Valdecasas; the founding of the "Agrupación al Servicio de la República" by Marañón, Ortega and Pérez de Ayala; the proclamation of the Republic in 1931 – all served as background for the generation's activity. Politics and literature were alive and we lived them at the University.

A group coalesced there (and not in the School of Letters, but in the Law School), and promptly carried out the ritual act : the publication of a review. José Antonio Maravall, Leopoldo Panero, José Ramón Senteiro and Manuel Díaz Berrio edited it, giving it a simple but ambitious title : *Nueva Revista.* It turned out to be a sequel to the avant-garde, well-written and moderate in tone, but it was not so "new" as the title indicated. It was inevitable : the work and the prestige of the writers of '25 were at their peak and it hardly seemed possible to avoid their influence. At that time, Rafael Alberti was still alluding disdainfully to poets "who write verses to their girl friends" and Luis Rosales heard him with surprise and embarrassment, as he thought about how much of that sort of poetry he was carrying around in his pocket. The young men of the *Nueva Revista* were intelligent and well educated. As followers of Ortega, and nourished by the best poetry of the time, they gave the publication a special, serious and mature tone.

In 1930, Ildefonso-Manuel Gil and I, with others not so young, and differently oriented, brought out *Brújula,* of which there were four issues. The inherent differences among the staff and the disagreements among the editors forced us to discontinue it. Shortly thereafter, Gil and I published the most fleeting of literary papers, *Boletín Ultimo,* which was published only once and had only one subscriber : Juan Ramón Jiménez.

In the provinces, there was an uninterrupted birth-and-death sequence of groups and reviews. Among the more attractive ones were *Murta,* in Valencia, with Rafael Duyos and Ramón Faraldo (who was still using his first last name : Descalzo) : *Isla,* in Cádiz, directed by Pedro Pérez Clotet, who also published an attractive series of poetry pamphlets; *Atalaya,* in Navarra, with the brothers Alfonso and Francisco Rodríguez Aldave; *Ddooss,* in Valladolid, with José María Luelmo and Francisco Pina; and later, *Agora,* in Albacete, directed by José S. Serna.

In 1935 *Hoja literaria* appeared in Madrid, and with it the impetuous and enthusiastic trio of Enrique Azcoaga, Antonio Sánchez Barbudo and Arturo Serrano Plaja. More political and less cautious, they brought a marked polemical accent to the language and the attitude of the generation. And in 1935 also, Gabriel Celaya became known with *Marea del silencio,* his first book, signed not by the pseudonym that has since made him famous, but with his real name : Rafael Mújica.

Miguel Hernández, "the boy-wonder of Orihuela", had begun his career under almost fabulous auspices. His poems and his "auto sacramental" *Quien te ha visto y quien te ve o sombra de lo que fuiste* appeared, respectively, in *Revista de Occidente* and *Cruz y Raya.* Ortega heard about him; Bergamín published his work; Juan Ramón dedicated enthusiastic lines to him in *El Sol;* the poets of the generation of '25 – Lorca, Aleixandre, Alberti – were his friends and encouraged him.

The generation of '36 arrived treading on the heels of the avant-garde writers, and as the difference in age was not great, nor were their intentions and assumptions, the two generations were easily welded together. The younger men accepted the mature ones without objection. That is to say : their work, not their leadership. Neither Miguel Hernández, nor Luis Rosales, nor the Panero brothers felt that they were merely continuers, even though they accepted and recognized the talent of their predecessors. The best way "to follow in their footsteps" would consist in being faithful to their own personal way of perceiving poetry and approaching artistic creation.

Admiration does not exclude lucidity; Leopoldo Panero, who knew Jorge Guillén's first *Cántico* by heart, neither was, nor wanted to be, nor could be, in his poetry, a disciple. Guillenian in his fervor, he nevertheless did not let his admiration draw him into imitation, which might have led him astray and perhaps destroyed him. The epigones arrived later, but who could be interested in the tiresome secretions of servile imitators? They survived . . . Why not? . . . There were the calico Lorquians, pasteboard surrealists, cheap Aleixandrians, Guillenians devoid of the joy of life . . . Bah !

In 1934 Ildefonso-Manuel Gil and I published *Literatura.* The title implied taking a stand against certain ideas of the preceding generation. Gerardo Diego, its spokesman, had carried to an extreme the opposition between poetry and literature, condemning everything that appeared to be contaminated by the latter. His condemnation struck us as disproportionate and sterile. Under the pretext of purity, life, which is essentially ambiguous, chaotic and impure, was to be relegated to the "open, mixed, murky field of literature".

Literatura was a meeting place for the two generations; our determination to not form too tight a circle was evident not only in the attention we gave to things foreign (Max Jacob and Louis Parrot collaborated in the journal), but in the reviews and criticism of works by writers who were almost always on the sidelines of critical commentary, such as Ramón J. Sender and José María Pemán, both members of the constellation I have called "extravagant", with respect to the nucleus of the generation of 1925.

Soon, *Literatura* began to publish a series of books called *P.E.N. Colección;* some people read "Pen", and translated it as *Colección La Pluma.* But what it meant was Poets, Essayists, Novelists. We were trying to eliminate the predominance, almost the exclusivity, of the poets, by considering as equally legitimate and deserving of encouragement the efforts of prose writers. In the collections of books published by the avant-garde (*Litoral, Mediodía*), the poets always predominated; in ours we opted for equal rights, and the first two volumes were narrations in prose, one of them the fragrant *San Alejo,* by Benjamín Jarnés. Thanks to this tendency, books as notable as *Meditaciones políticas,* by Angel Sánchez Rivero – the unjustly forgotten critic – and José Ferrater Mora's first book were able to be included.

The generation of '25 and that of '36 had intertwined and established contact in different ways and through different channels. Leopoldo Panero and Maravall collaborated in *El Sol;* Ildefonso-Manuel Gil and Enrique Azcoaga in *Luz;* Vivanco, Rosales and Muñoz Rojas in *Cruz y Raya;* Germán Bleiberg, Hernández, Maravall and I collaborated in the *Revista de Occidente.* The one did not exclude the other, naturally, and in theory, these and other publications were open to everyone. The writers of the avant-garde were cordial and generous toward the younger men : Guillermo de Torre gave them access to the literary pages of *Diario de Madrid* and, later, to Spanish-American reviews; José Bergamín welcomed them to *Cruz y Raya* and published *Abril,* by Luis Rosales; Fernando Vela accepted the new arrivals in the *Revista de Occidente* and the newspapers in his charge; in the excellent *Colección Héroe,* Manuel Altolaguirre published Juan Panero's, Luis Felipe Vivanco's and Germán Bleiberg's first books; Pedro Salinas, through his professorship and in private was as much friend as teacher, and when *La voz a ti debida* was published, his students repaid him handsomely.

Somewhat later, the School of Letters was another focus for the activities of the generation. What a faculty! There were Ortega, Morente, Zubiri, Montesinos, Salinas . . . And among the students, besides several already mentioned, were María Zambrano, Antonio Rodríguez Huéscar, Julián Marías ... The review published by the School of Letters could stand comparison with any of the reviews mentioned above.

As for tertulias, they were everywhere : at the "Ateneo", in coffee-houses, and in private homes. On Sunday afternoons, at María Zambrano's; almost every afternoon at the house of the affable Benjamín Jarnés. Even before the War broke out, a substantial group of writers used to gather at the Café Lyon. Affinities and differences determined groupings and regroupings, as well as our approach to the established writers.

Toward 1930, some of us met and soon felt the charm of Eugenio d'Ors, an admirable teacher; among other things, he revealed to us the secrets of modern art. In the virgin field of Spanish art criticism, his talent and passion – his controlled passion – were hard to believe. He broke the ice of the hirsute Celtiberianism exalted by academic types and outlined the map of modern

13

esthetic currents. His *Cézanne*, his commentaries on esthetic problems, passed from hand to hand, and from them we learned to recognize the gracefulness and beauty which the purists attacked.

Unamuno let himself be heard, tireless, a lofty example of independence in the face of everything. He was not only the heterodox of orthodoxies, but the heterodox of heterodoxy, the opponent of conformities and of non-conformities that in the last analysis proposed a conformity no less rigid; conformities in reverse. If Ortega's call was for order, discipline and rigorous control, Unamuno incited rebellion, protest against external pressures, from wherever they might come, against all attempts at regimentation. The one and the other, internal discipline and protest, were necessary to maintain spiritual and other liberties. Don Miguel's return to Spain in 1930 and the fervent reception with which he was honored was, unquestionably, one of the instances of exaltation and coinciding of generations.

Nevertheless, I would say that Ortega's influence was the greater. The generation of '36 is saturated with Orteganism : María Zambrano, Rodríguez Huéscar, Julián Marías, Pedro Laín . . . and not far removed, José Luis Aranguren and José Ferrater Mora, all declare themselves as disciples. Ortega was the most heeded of the distinguished writers. We read him in the newspaper every morning; we read his books, which we anxiously awaited. Never, perhaps, has any other writer in our language, in Spain and elsewhere, enjoyed so much rational admiration, nor influenced youth as did Ortega, up to 1936.

He was stimulating even when one disagreed with him; for example, when he claimed that Debussy was a more "select" musician than Beethoven. Sometimes we took what seemed useful from his statements, and even misreading him we managed to understand him fairly well. For young people, *La deshumanización del arte* was not, as some hasty readers suppose, a breviary of aloofness from everyday life. The generation of '36 accepted the book's diagnosis of a tendency, but it neither utilized it as a guide for creating, nor even believed that the word "dehumanization" was exact when applied to that tendency. But, apart from this and other disagreements, how many Ortegan ideas we assimilated, how many attitudes and techniques of work we acquired!

In the early days, the generation of '36, later so nomadic, ventured out of Spain less than the previous generation; on the other hand, it was not less familiar with the highways and byways of its country. With the *Misiones pedagógicas*, created by don Fernando de los Ríos for the diffusion of culture through towns and villages that had been, until then, forgotten; with *La Barraca*, the mobile theatre directed by Federico García Lorca, that carried to remote corners the *Entremeses* of Cervantes and the "auto sacramental" of *La vida es sueño*, among other works; with all this, young men from twenty to twenty-five years of age – Azcoaga, Eugenio Mediano Flores, Ernesto G. Da Cal – made contact with the Spanish people.

Others made contact by travelling alone or in a group through different areas. In the summer of 1934, Maravall, Gil and I retraced on foot the route of El Cid, thus following out the Modernist idea that one's country was meaningful once one got to know it. On that trip, full of odd incidents that are not pertinent here, three Spaniards born outside Castilla agreed on their passionate admiration for the basic character of that region. An account of it appeared in the essay of the Valencian Maravall, "Castilla o la moral de la creación", published shortly thereafter in the *Revista de Occidente*.

The later travels of Camilo José Cela – perhaps the youngest of the men of '36 and the last to be incorporated into the main wave of the generation – are in the same vein, eager for knowledge, dictated by the desire to know the nature of the people who are really the foundation of the country in their daily work, to know those whom Unamuno called the silent ones of intrahistory.

The first of the generation to achieve total recognition had been Miguel Hernández, but because of his rapid and widespread success, he was seen as belonging to the previous generation, operating in and with it, rather like a younger brother. *Abril,* by Luis Rosales, seemed quite different. His voice resounded in another way, and his poetry echoed unexpected affiliations, with writers such as Fernando de Herrera. Disgusted as he is by the formalist and escapist excesses of the postwar period, the present-day reader may have to expend considerable effort to understand what that book meant at the time. By way of Bleiberg-Ridruejo, both of whom Rosales influenced directly, the most valuable expression of subsequent Garcilasism derived from him.

The Café Lyon and the Rosales-Vivanco-Panero group served as a bridge between the years of '36 and '39. Among the youthful literary tertulias before the war, the one at the Lyon was the only one that was revived, considerably changed, at the end of the war. In its second stage, José Suárez Carreño, Gerardo Diego and José María de Cossío, with the survivors, frequented it. It soon merged with the circle of don Manuel Machado, and from that came the reunion of three generations, and relationships with such interesting types as the great actor Ricardo Calvo and the poet don Antonio de Zayas.

The congeniality and cordiality of don Manuel, a mixture of what is best in a Sevillian and most distinguished in a Madrileño – within the popular sphere – served as the binding element. I do not recall whether it was his or Cossío's idea to establish a literary academy along the lines of those of the seventeenth and eighteenth centuries. They thought that in the sullen Madrid of 1940 it would be healthy to shorten distances among writers and to get them in the habit of coming together, to recapture something of the lost camaraderie that once existed among writers.

Eduardo Llosent y Marañón, director of the Museum of Modern Art, offered his office so that the academy might hold its sessions there. After some discussion, it was given the name *Musa, musae*. This invocation to the improbable ethereal elements made sense. Nothing grandiloquent, nothing alluding to spatial nor temporal qualities would have been suitable, in naming the fraternity; it was a question, necessarily, of suggesting a place that was free of any connection with circumstances.

In one of the sessions something important happened, from the generational point of view. One afternoon, in the antechamber of the museum, there erupted the grave and virile voice of Leopoldo Panero, to recite in slow impassioned lines a canto of love. Those present, some forty persons, were from the first moment overcome by the strength, sincerity and beauty of the words. Those assembled felt at once that something great was happening before their eyes. Until he began to recite, Panero was, for the majority of those gathered there, a nice boy "who wrote verse"; when he had finished – after long seconds of silence that indicated the depth of emotion and surprise – he was, for everyone, a poet.

This moment, rather late in relation to those that revealed Miguel Hernández and Luis Rosales, stands next to the explosion of *La familia de Pascual Duarte*, with which Camilo José Cela brought down the barriers of prudent novel-writing and made his way into literature through the front door. Leopoldo's appearance made me think, through "unconscious cerebration", and notwithstanding so many obvious differences of time and place, of Zorrilla's appearance at the foot of Larra's tomb. Here, the tomb would be that of Miguel, in Alicante.

Miguel, who met such an untimely death; and Juan Panero, whose life was cut short even sooner, at twenty-nine; Panero's poetic gift, far from precocious, matured slowly and was hardly beginning to bear fruit when he perished, victim of a stupid accident on a Leonese highway, a short distance from his home. Juan lived exaltedly, surrendering himself unconditionally to life. He was lost in many things, but he found himself in love and in poetry. He put writing aside for later, for after having enjoyed the delights in which he was immersing himself. Everything would come at its proper time; there was tenderness and there was gracefulness; feeling and the ability to express it in words. Everyone who knew him trusted in him and in the future : that tense life that would end in the creation of a work full of richness. But death did not give him time. It swooped down on him and carried him off, leaving hardly a sample of what he was capable of doing.

He died in the midst of the Civil War. That war which forever separated and united the men of the generation of '36 : it made them actors when others did not go beyond being spectators. The postwar period saw them fighting again, fighting here and there to save themselves, collectively and individually. As a generation, one could say of them what Gertrude Stein said to Hemingway : you are a lost generation. As a group, it suffered from ineffectualness and an awareness of inferiority. Perhaps for that very reason we are united; it is that strange solidarity which – personal achievements aside – we might call the solidarity of failure.

University of Texas

The Generation of 1936 ...
for the Second Time*

GUILLERMO DE TORRE

Why all this persistence in grouping present day writers by generation? Why, for some years now, has even the most insignificant writer wanted to be registered in one generational compartment or another? It seems that this method is now reaching certain abusive limits. Are not those of us who have tried in recent years to apply this method to literature guilty of such exaggeration even while adhering to selected norms? We at least took into account the natural intervals that all generations have – periods of fifteen, thirty and forty-five years corresponding respectively to dominance, stabilization, and retreat – and we also were careful to consider as generations only those offering a complete physiognomy (i.e., those generations that brought changes of undeniable transcendence). But nowadays generations are invented whenever it strikes the fancy of any group (especially poets), in Spain as well as in Spanish America.

In Hispanic letters, the first time this concept was properly applied was when Pedro Salinas, as a summary of a course that he was then teaching at the University of Madrid, gave an after-dinner talk at the P.E.N. Club (which was later published in *Revista de Occidente,* December, 1935, and also in *Literatura española siglo XX,* Mexico, 1941). Basing himself on Hans Jeschke (whose book on *Die Generation von 1898 in Spanien,* 1934, had not yet been translated; the book he dedicated to Ganivet is still untranslated) as well as on the eight factors which Julius Petersen used as determinants of a generation, Salinas succeeded in demonstrating the existence of the widely-discussed group. Group? (Individuality, rather, since the name emerged, like an armed Minerva, from Azorín's head, who, however, has not treated the subject in the unified book that was needed, dispersing instead his campaigns in articles and giving information and documents to other writers; first to Werner Mullert, then to Ramón Gómez de la Serna.) Baroja, for his part, never accepted – given his irreducible anarchistic temperament – that generation's existence, and both Unamuno and Valle-Inclán were completely indifferent to it, in the same manner that Maeztu seemed to include it in the general excommunication that he made of his youth. But there

*First published in *Insula* (July-August, 1965), and then collected in Guillermo de Torre, *Al pie de las letras* (Buenos Aires, 1967). Permission granted by author. Translated by D.P.T. and Carol Dana.

17

is no need for me to give here the trajectory of the concept of generation in Spain or in any other literature, since I have indicated the milestones in other essays.

What was the first critical attempt to establish a literary generation of 1936? It occurred about twenty years ago and since it went unnoticed in Spain, as did my response to it – apparently due to the lack of communication at the time – I consider the following facts essential. Homero Serís published an article entitled "The Spanish Generation of 1936", in *Books Abroad*, XIX (1945), later reproduced in Spanish in a pamphlet at Syracuse University. I responded immediately to this article with one of my own, "La supuesta generación española de 1936", in *Cabalgata* (Buenos Aires; no. 1, October 1, 1945), refuting Serís' arguments politely but energetically.

This industrious scholar of Spanish literature, who belonged to the illustrious group of the Centro de Estudios Históricos of Madrid, went to the United States after the Spanish Civil War where he has continued to dedicate his working days to a task that is as thankless as it is worthwhile : tirelessly accumulating index cards (to say memoranda or slips would be a better description of his breed, in the style of Nicolás Antonio). But undoubtedly the mere title of bibliographer is inadequate for him. Let it be known, in any case, that Homero Serís practices this impersonal science or skill in an extremely original and individual way. He does not limit himself to cataloguing in a routine manner. First of all, he creates new thematic sections : he is the first, for example, to insert a section on "Literary Generations", another on "Spanish Culture Among Exiles"; then he comments and even polemicizes fearlessly and flawlessly . . . Of similar nature, and truly an exceptional work, are the two volumes – the ones printed so far – of his *Manual de bibliografía de literatura española* (1948), published by the Centro de Estudios Hispánicos, which he created, of the aforementioned Syracuse University (before moving finally to the Hispanic Society of America in New York, which has published his *Nuevo ensayo de una biblioteca española de libros raros y curiosos*). In contrast to the inevitably dry reading that burdens ordinary bibliographical collections, Homero Serís' work is exceedingly provocative and pleasant. Why this uniqueness? Because its author adroitly infuses a keen spirit and a lively polemical intent in every page.

Is there not good reason to think then that these were the qualities that impelled Homero Serís to undertake the heroic task of "inventing" a Spanish generation of 1936? Let us not forget the moment : it was the time when people thought it still possible to resolve injustices by polemical means through slashing literary attacks. Logically obsessed by the recent struggle, Homero Serís began his argument in the following way : "Just as a war was the cause and the antecedent to the crystallization in Spain of the so-called Generation of 1898, so has another war created a new generation that I would call the Generation of 1936." From this, it is obvious that the initial pretext for adducing the existence of a literary generation could not be more extra-literary. "Ideas are not born of fists", wrote Antonio Machado, after 1918. Besides, is not a war with such special characteristics – not to say abominable, the memory of which should be buried once and for all – the underlying cause for interminable schisms and divisions, rather than the source of transcendent conglomerates and assemblages? But in Professor Serís' judgment the meetings held in Madrid, during the war, by a certain "Alliance of Intellectuals" acquired transcendent characteristics. And after quoting from publications of the period which, apart from their legitimate purpose, had significance only for the occasion – i.e., as combat weapons rather than literary works – he traced an account of the writers who, in his opinion, formed the Generation of 1936. But it happens that all of them were not born as writers precisely during the war; they already appeared firmly linked to other generational groups. It is enough to point out, for example, that, among the poets, he begins with Moreno Villa (who emerged in 1913), Antonio Espina (1916), León Felipe (1920), Federico García Lorca (1921), plus those who by common agreement have been designated as the "Generation of 1925" or "1927" – Guillén, Salinas, Alberti, etc. – and ends with Miguel Hernández, the only one who could be included in the "Generation of 1936", although strictly speaking he had already appeared on the scene three years before. The differences are even greater between the only two novelists that Serís presents to us as belonging to the Generation forged by him : Benjamín Jarnés (born in 1888) and Ramón Sender (in 1902) are not contemporaries – since they are not the same age – nor do they resemble each other in esthetic sensibility, and they represent two radically opposed ways of understanding and executing the novel. No less astonishing was his linking of the only two names that he proposed with respect to drama : Jacinto Grau and Alejandro Casona. While the author of *Entre llamas* (his first work, 1905) belongs to the declining years of the "1898" movement, the author of *La sirena varada* (1934), with no visible connection to a specific generation, appears quite a few years later[1]; they both have, in addition, very different esthetics. Nor do I see, finally, any greater affinity among the three essayists that Serís mentions (María Zambrano, José Bergamín, and Guillermo de Torre).

No, my dear Mr. Serís (I then concluded in my reply, cited above); no, despite your generous and good intentions, a Spanish Generation of 1936 does not exist, nor anything like it. The fact is that a generation is not invented artificially, nor is it created by critical parthenogenesis, no matter how much cleverness and flexibility one uses to apply Petersen's rules. That grouping could have been valuable, at best, as an incomplete index of Spanish writers in exile. Equating literature with politics soon proved to be impracticable. It served to confirm once more – in the words Henri Peyre – that "strict equivalence between segments of history and phases of literary history falsifies our perspectives".

Neither the War of 1914 nor the War of 1939 really revealed anything (as I have explained elsewhere), since their operative values already existed (or pre-existed) years before; what no one can doubt is that, in countries that fell victim to dictatorial upheavals, the Second World War left a number of European literatures submerged. The best way not to understand literary phenomena is to base them on extra-literary determinism (as in this case, war). (If it were a

---

[1]To confirm these dates, do not rely on the *Manual de bibliografía de la literatura española,* published by José Simón Díaz (1963). It would be futile. In the cited examples – and in various others – he does not include what really matters in situating an author chronologically : i.e., the dates of first editions. He goes by the dates of the last editions that he has found in circulation. This objection should be offset with the praise that all difficult bibliographical work, in theory, deserves.

question of social conditioning or the reflection of society, that would be different.)

But here we have the Generation of 1936 again raising its head, asking to be admitted to literary history. Or to be more accurate, although the date may be the same, the components and characteristics are now different.[2] The war is fortunately far away – though not so far away as some of us would prefer, in opposition to the reactionaries and fanatics – and this time the Generation of 1936 is presented to us, above all, with "a very praiseworthy feature : the desire for reconciliation among Spaniards". These are the words of my intimate friend Ricardo Gullón (in an article published in *Asomante, no. 1, 1959*), one of the writers most legitimately attributable to this disputed generation, and who has been trying to win for it critical recognition, which *Insula* now confirms. It is true that Ricardo Gullón began his article by asking : "Can one speak of a Spanish Generation of 1936 with any accuracy?" Actually he does not hide the fact that "the event which unites the generation is – paradoxically – the War", and while likewise recognizing that "as a consequence of the dispersal caused by the War, the generation today may seem to be divided into two groups", he nevertheless affirms that this division in reality "is an optical illusion" and "if such a separation does exist with respect to distance, it does not exist – save for exceptions – with respect to attitudes". Are some of the very few elements – apart from their highly noble aim of transcending the War and its schisms, that is, the desire to have people live together – which Gullón points out in the purely literary domain really the casual elements of a properly constituted generation? For example, the return to a certain tradition "full of fertile innovations" on the part of some poets (Rosales, Panero, Vivanco . . .), or the fusion of "the best vanguardist experiments with rigorously classical and even baroque forms" (Miguel Hernández). Gullón includes then the names of other authors – mostly poets – who emerged in the years immediately before and after the Civil War.

But we are scarcely given any details, with respect to the other literary genres. And it goes without saying that a generation fully worthy of the name cannot be defined by one literary mode of expression. Reacting years ago against that simplified trend – accepted idly by the majority – I ventured, a propos of García Lorca (in *El fiel de la balanza* and *La aventura estética de nuestra edad*) to broaden the scope of the Generation of 1927 by including equally significant figures, such as critics and essayists, novelists, playwrights, and even a few painters and sculptors. It would be appropriate to broaden it even further at different levels by bringing in philosophers and public figures, if we agree – as Ortega Gasset once wrote – that "a generation is not a handful of eminent men, nor simply the masses : it resembles more a new integral social body, with its elite and its crowd . . ."

It is not that significant names are missing from the lists that Gullón establishes of the writers making up the Generation of 1936, although those who were publicly known by that date are few : among the latter, he mentions Germán Bleiberg, Gabriel Celaya, Arturo Serrano Plaja, Enrique Azcoaga, José Antonio

[2]See the articles published in *Insula*, no. 224-225 (July-August, 1965).

Maravall, Antonio Sánchez Barbudo, María Zambrano, Rosa Chacel, José Ferrater Mora, and Gullón himself. But the majority listed by him only began to emerge during or after the War: Pedro Laín Entralgo, Julián Marías, Dionisio Ridruejo, José Antonio Gaya Nuño, Ernesto Da Cal, José Manuel Blecua, José Luis Cano, Ramón de Garcíasol, Francisco Ynduráin, José Suárez Carreño, Carlos Clavería, Antonio Rodríguez Huéscar . . . Gullón recognizes that "some names are missing", that others could be added, and that these "others" will see to it that the list is made complete. If Gullón does not include novelists, it is because they appear later, in the 40's, beginning with Cela and Carmen Laforet – in Spain – and Arturo Barea – among the writers in exile – while others in fact had published before 1936 (Max Aub, Francisco Ayala, Sender, Salazar Chapela), and a few much later (for example, Serrano Poncela).

We are dealing – somebody may say – with a generation of loose and flexible boundaries. This would not matter substantially, if there were clear points of similarity, or a certain possible common denominator. The list of names can always be extended or reduced; the latter will occur, as usual, after a few years; what is important however is that these men continue to exist as writers without giving in to other inclinations. It is unquestionable that some have produced or are producing significant works – as in the case of the essayists Aranguren, Laín Entralgo, Marías, Tovar, Tierno Galván – but it is more debatable to say that they form a generation in a strict sense and especially that the year 1936 could be their focal point.

What fascinations and dangers in the generational system, so alluring and yet so delicate to handle! I shall not be explicit here – there are too many details – on the necessary characteristics which must obtain in a clearly differentiated and innovative generation, one that is even polemical rather than "accumulative". Elsewhere I have set forth why, in my opinion, the biological factor is not important, why the author's year of physical birth rarely or exclusively matters (there are precocious writers and others slow to mature), but rather the year of his literary birth, which is determined by the publication of his first, or other decisive work, or of a unifying literary magazine, a manifesto, or a special public function; in short, by a public declaration of a peculiar state of sensibility or conscience, that is shared with other related elements. What is not enough, therefore, to give form and meaning to an authentic literary generation is the mere coincidence of time, of a vague common objective, or of any other external factor.

II

A SYMPOSIUM OF VIEWS

Introduction

In this section will be found perspectives that further contribute to a discussion of the encompassing problems relating to the existence of the Generation of 1936. The papers collected here were presented at the Symposium of November, 1967, convened in honour of Homero Serís on the Syracuse University campus and dedicated to the subject of which he was the original formulator. For that open forum, new views were solicited on this broad issue that vitally affects a whole generation of intellectuals and writers.

The response which emerges in the following papers is the result of a human as much as a literary and ideological confrontation, and the writers represented here, from both sides of the Atlantic, seem rather to agree with Ricardo Gullón's gestures of conciliation than with Guillermo de Torre's reluctance to accept this new mood as a basis for constituting the generation in question. As viewed by the commentators in this section, "Generation of 1936" is not an easily definable and demonstrable set of literary-historical facts – restricted and frozen in time – but rather a dynamic and evolving concept that, because of the special circumstances produced by the Spanish Civil War, must be based partly on a perspectivistic reconstruction of history. In seeking to identify the authentic moral and literary postures, multiple modes of inquiry are employed : introspection, analysis vis à vis other members of the group, and scrutiny in literary works of the writer's moral and human response to the turmoil imposed by events. It should be noted that such techniques of study are germane principally to the subjective genres (poetry and the personal essay) rather than to the objective ones (fiction, drama).

At any rate, we believe that the existence of the "Generation of 1936" has been further strengthened by the arguments put forward in the following pages, although we likewise recognize that its complete, historically valid, configuration is something that only future studies will provide.

Characteristics of the Thought of the Spanish Generation of 1936*

JOSE LUIS ARANGUREN

. . . Naturally, it displeases me profoundly that we must call ourselves the Generation of 1936, but what displeases me more is that the year 1936 occurred, and whether we like it or not, we are men whose intellectual life, great or small, undistinguished or brilliant, began in that year of 1936 or as a consequence of it. Therefore, we have to accept that designation, if we really exist as a generation. And if we really exist as a generation, we were given birth and we remain marked forever by that event, the event of the War. To deny it would be to run away from ourselves, and in this respect (later we shall examine it in a little more detail), I believe that our significance beyond the realm of literature depends on the fact that we do not resemble the majority of the great intellectuals – to whom we can now refer as "sacred monsters", – who placed themselves "au-dessus de la mêlée". None of us has placed himself "au-dessus de la mêlée". Those of us on one side or the other may have fallen often in error, but we all have experienced the war, and that is what characterizes us. In that sense, it seems to me that Juan Marichal's last prologue to Azaña's *Obras completas* illuminates well what I mean. We subscribe – I do not say in every respect nor do I say that we subscribe at all to Azaña's general attitude – but we indeed subscribe, we have already subscribed with our own lives, to being a part of the bloody and tragic event, of the far from frivolous event (as someone once said of it) which was the Spanish Civil War. . . .We should not forget that those of us born around 1910 are the oldest members of that generation, and the problem of the demarcation should not be treated with a criterion that is excessively mathematically chronological. In any case, the limits would have to be determined, but it is undeniable that, with reference to age, we are the oldest of the group.

But there are others who were as marked by the War of 1936 as we were, those who already had, let us say, their use of reason, those who were able to confront the events and judge them, and to make choices, to make choices blindly, and then later to correct their mistakes, because – as we shall see immediately – this has been one of the dominant characteristics of the Generation of 1936. But all of us who are included, all of us who in one way or another were "militarized"

*Originally published in *Symposium* XXII (1968); translated by D. P. T.

– in the broadest sense of that word – by the year 1936, all of us belong to that generation, whether we call it that or something else. Those excluded are the ones who were too old to be militarized – now with its narrow meaning – and the ones who were too young, those whose consciousness of 1936 consists of the jarring collision between their dim, early childhood war experiences and a superimposed rationalization offered by the Franco Régime and by the Learned Clergy of the Régime's Holy Mother Church. These are the ones, in my judgment, who fall outside the generation. Included are those of us who have had to assume, and who will have to assume forever, the burdensome consequences of that tragic event in Spanish History and in our own personal history.

Now, among the men of the Generation of 1936, there have been two somewhat different attitudes and both of course equally respectable. There are those people who have remained as faithful as possible to the attitude that was decided by the very occurrence of the War. No one has remained entirely faithful. We are in that respect very Unamunian – we are our own contradiction, we continually contribute to our own contradiction. In any case, there have been some who have done this on a lesser scale than others, and though it may be pure chance (or perhaps it isn't), the fact pleases me – and seems to prove my point – that my dear friend José María Valverde is to speak immediately after me, because I, one of the oldest members of the Generation of 1936, in contrast, have always had the disposition to look not to the past nor even to the event itself which determined our lives but rather to the future. A rather slight accomplishment, undoubtedly, but if I have done anything of merit it has been to make our generation accessible to the generations that followed. On the other hand, José María Valverde seems already to announce in the very title of his paper that his attitude has been a complementary one in extending the friendly hand of youth to those of us who are older. In this manner – and I beg your indulgence that at this moment I have exemplified "in anima vili" (I refer to myself) – both of us have served symbolically as a bridge. But our whole generation has been a bridge between one group and another, between those who preceded us and those who followed us.

That would be, in my opinion, the essential content which determines and distinguishes us from those who are older and those who are younger (but I trust that in later discussions we will clarify this concept of the limits to the generation). Neither the first nor the second group was as marked by the War as we were, precisely because we found ourselves in a moment of intellectual receptivity, unlike our elders who already possessed an established mentality and a point of view towards things that had developed over the years, and unlike the very young, the children, who did not yet know on what to rely. This is the way we were formed. We are creatures of 1936 and we have to accept it no matter how much it causes us to suffer.

What are, then, the characteristics of this generation, or whatever term you may want to give it? I believe that its fundamental characteristics consist in the fact (and here I shall borrow a word very accurately used by Pedro Laín Entralgo, I think, although in a different context and for a different purpose) that all of us of the Generation of 1936 are in one way or another "driven" men : men driven into jail, men driven into exile, men driven from their university chairs, a few of them "driven" – and by no means am I thinking of myself at this moment – because they lived impelled by their boldness; others, "driven" from life itself, like Miguel Hernández. This, it seems to me, is an ineradicable trait of our generation. We should observe that even those who do not appear to have been physically dislocated, those who appear to have accepted the historical occurrence that made us what we are inside of Spain, nevertheless also feel uprooted in their internal lives, and it seems to me that is what Ildefonso-Manuel Gil calls attention to. In that withdrawal into private life, there is a dislodgement and an awareness that it was impossible to live in public life, which we as humans can never renounce. This retreat into one's inner being begins then to form, and that is another manner of being ejected from historical existence, from a collective existence. This is one of our essential characteristics.

Another trait, which I mentioned earlier, is that of our being changeable. We are all changeable. There have been other thinkers who were not. There have been others, like Ortega y Gasset, who have always maintained a strong desire to demonstrate that they had always been the same and that they had anticipated themselves in everything that was later said, etc., etc. With us the opposite is true : we know that we are always changing, we know that we do not have a personality that is sculptured, like a statue; we know that we are completely inconstant and that it is our destiny, and that we shall not be able to strip ourselves of that characteristic. Our being changeable is in the realm of ideology, as you all well know. All members of the generation have changed ideologically, in one direction or another. To repeat, this trait is basic in our lives.

Likewise, the characteristic of being subjected to what we could call "cross pressures" – to use an expression of modern sociology – conflicting pressures in our internal life. Think, for example, about the very important function that the fact has had of our being Catholic, but not of the Catholicism represented by the Spanish Church of the Franco Régime. An essential point of our generation, it seems to me, is this existing and not existing, this finding ourselves divided, severed, in our inner beings. I believe that this trait is very closely related to the others.

Ours is by no means a triumphal generation. This was true of the Generation of 1898, which after all was indeed successful. The Generation of 1910 was also clearly an exalted generation : the confidence, the magnificence which it possessed, even in speaking, the rhetorical tone of a Eugenio d'Ors, the pontifical certainty of Ortega; all that we lack. We can lament it, or others may consider it to be one of our very many faults, but the truth is that this is so, and we have to confess it, precisely because we have not been confident of success, precisely because we know that our mission has not been to proclaim a truth which everyone repeats as disciples. Not at all. Our character has been very different. If we have contributed something positive to those who follow, it has been an ethical or moral sense. By that I do not mean that all of us have been very moral or very ethical, and at this moment it makes no difference to me (or almost no difference) that you are thinking about those whom you consider more strictly ethical rather than about those whom you consider less so, because we are all tied together by a bad conscience. None of us has a clear conscience. A few will feel more guilty because in some manner they are collaborationists and they know it, and not one of them feels comfortable (I am speaking of course of the authentic intellectuals), not one of them feels comfortable in that position. This is true of others of us as well, because even in the cases where we have broken with the Régime, we know that we have not done as much as we could have. We all live with an internal tormentor, and it seems to me that this is another characteristic of our generation and surely the most noble of all and the one which you will esteem most highly, in its finest example.

You are probably thinking that I am saying absolutely nothing about what it seems I was supposed to speak, that is, about "The Characteristics of the Thought of the Generation of 1936". In reality, our generation's thought is too immersed in our existence for us not to feel obligated to give primacy to our installation in life, in our national life, in the historical life of our country and for our installation in life not to have stamped on us a character greater than what we think and what we say. At any rate, this is what is translated and is made evident in the superstructure – as a Marxist would say – of our ideas. Let us take the case of a great thinker who is with us here, José Mariá (as he is known to his friends) Ferrater-Mora, who is always revising what he has done, who continually has things at his disposal which end up not being utilized. Since he does not write different books, he goes back to the same ones, and in this process he is perhaps subtly ensnared, because his work continues to be the same but it is really no longer the same. You can see, therefore, how our being changeable is translated into our literary work, and how our work does nothing but make our installation in life evident, transparent, and exposed to view.

My own life, it seems to me, is characterized by an evolution which is perhaps more confessional than José Ferrater-Mora's but in my opinion more or less equally true. And all of us, I believe, all of us are this way on another level of thought. Or to put it in more conventional terms, we of the generation have drawn from many philosophies : beginning with what came to be "unamunismo" and "orteguismo" and the philosophical currents approximately contemporaneous with them; later, the currents which still prevail among the younger people, Marxism, either in its orthodox or heterodox strains (and of course Marxism *per se* is worth much more in its heterodoxy than in its orthodoxy); other philosophical influences which we can simply call Anglosaxon. That is to say, we find ourselves at a crossroads, we are a crossroads generation. (It is not by mere chance that José Ferrater-Mora included this word in the title of one of his books.) Thus you can say, depending on whether you think well of us or not, that we are a pivotal generation, or that we are an ephemeral or transitional generation. In any case, we are for good or ill thus constituted, and we are obligated to accept ourselves as we are.

It is for me a moving fact that the first public event, to my knowledge, of remembrance, of recognition, of some kind of celebration of the "Generation of 1936", the first open forum, has come to be held precisely here, in the United States. All of you know that in Spain today there is not a very favorable image of America, but there is – also to borrow the expression of another title – "the other America", and it is to that America that we, some of the members of the Generation of 1936, owe our being together here, we who have been, in one manner or another, driven from the Spain in which we would rather be, and where in spirit we reside.

The University of California, Santa Barbara

On the Validity of
the Concept of "Generation"*

JOSE FERRATER-MORA

Professor Marichal is absolutely right in proposing this more general question[1], since all those who have participated in this colloquium have spoken of the Generation of 1936, and have thus taken for granted that the expression "generation of . . ." is meaningful.

Is such an assumption acceptable? Is it legitimate to talk about generations, and specifically about literary generations? These are difficult questions to answer, for the fact is that no definite criteria can be laid down which are acceptable to everyone concerned – to literary critics and historians of literature –. It would seem, therefore, that we would do well to rule out the notion of a generation. On the other hand, several people have talked at length about the Generation of 1936 and have been able to say something significant about it, so that the expression "generation of . . ." has proved to be useful. I am reluctant to believe that they have lied shamelessly, or that they possess such extraordinary hypnotic powers as to convince all of us that there is something that does not exist.

Perhaps the best course to take in this respect is to admit that there is something to be said about a literary generation, and at the same time to take the concept of a "generation" *cum grano salis*. Accordingly, the notion of a "generation" may be handled as one of those concepts which, in the words of a contemporary philosopher (Wittgenstein), have no clear "edges" or "borders", and, therefore, are not meant to be "defined" in any strict way. The concept of a generation, and in particular of a literary generation, may be vague, and still remain useful.

People who speak of a generation usually refer to some kind of "establishment". It is only normal that the ones who speak of a particular generation are its members; it helps to identify them historically. This self-identification is taken up as a sign of existence by authors of literary histories, and by the students who are supposed to consult these histories. All this is, as it were, in the nature of things.

*Originally published in *Symposium,* XXII (1968); translated by Constance Sullivan, with revisions by the author.

[1]Professor Juan Marichal, serving as moderator of the round-table discussion held as part of the Symposium of "The Generation of 1936" (Syracuse University, November 11, 1967) proposed that Ferrater-Mora give his views on "the historical or historiographical validity of the concept of generation" (Editors' Note).

Now, how is it that the expression "the Spanish literary Generation of 1936" has become acceptable as designating an historical fact?

To begin with, some members of the so-called "Generation of 1936" are gathered here to talk about themselves – or, what amounts to the same thing, some writers have gathered here and have begun to speak of themselves as belonging to the generation of 1936. This is a contingent fact. Let us assume, for instance, that Professor Aranguren had stayed in Santa Barbara, or that he had not been violently expelled from his university chair, or simply that he would have refused to concern himself with the question of whether there is or not a literary generation of 1936 in Spain. Let us assume, furthermore, that no one else would have attended this colloquium. Would then the notion "Generation of 1936" gain the same relatively wide circulation which it seems to be attaining at present? I doubt it very much; self-identification seems to be a necessary requisite for literary "existence". If people do not feel that they "belong", then it is very unlikely that they will "belong". We may safely conclude, then, that the notion of some particular literary generation is, so to speak, a "self-engendered fact".

This fact, however, is not a result of a completely arbitrary decision by a group of people concerned. There must surely be some reason why some people feel that they may belong to a particular literary generation.

I will deal with this question in the form of some questions specifically addressed to Professor Aranguren. I agree with most of what he has said, but not with everything that he has said, for otherwise there would be no colloquium. In any case, I agree with Professor Aranguren (and also with Professor Gil) that if there is an historical axis of the literary generation of 1936, it is the Spanish Civil War which began in 1936. The question is now, however : what would have happened if there had been no war, or such other epoch-making event? I acknowledge that this is to suppose a great deal; specifically it amounts to introducing what philosophers call "a counter-factual conditional", namely to assume that there might not have happened what happened, or that something happened which did not happen. Yet I feel that counter-factual conditionals are not totally irrelevant for the understanding of human history, including literary history. So, then, let us suppose that there had been no Civil War in Spain in 1936. Could we still speak of the Generation of 1936? It seems rather doubtful, and in this respect I completely agree with Professor Aranguren. He has not asserted first that there is a literary generation of 1936, and asked later what historical basis there is for the existence of such a generation; rather he has first reminded us of a particular, although momentous, event which took place in 1936, and has used it as a basis for historically "locating" this generation. The members of the latter have gathered and have identified themselves as "generationally determined" by the afore-mentioned historical event. This has happened with the Generation of 1936 in a much more clear and self-conscious way than it happened with the members of the so-called Generation of 1898. There was also a resounding historical event in 1898, but this event did not exert, as far as I know, an impact on the members of the generation of 1898 comparable to that of the 1936–1939 Civil War on the members of the Generation of 1936. I am almost tempted to say that we owe to the 1936 Civil War the fact that there is a Generation of 1936. To be sure, I am also tempted to say something like : "How wonderful would it have been that no Generation of 1936 could possibly exist, since that would mean that we would have been spared the Civil War of 1936 !"

Under all these conditions, there is no harm in going on talking about the Generation of 1936. When all this is granted, however, some questions must be raised, and among them the question of what makes this generation different from any other in more than the fact of its temporal location. (As to its spatial location, the answer must run thus : "Scattered all over the world.")

I basically agree with Professor Aranguren that the Generation of 1936, and in particular its essayists (but also its poets and novelists in so far as they bring some type of thought into their literary productions) is somewhat different from the preceding generations – from, say, the Generation of 1927, and from the one preceding the latter, which could be the Generation of 1916, 1917 or 1918 (I am already at a loss in the tabulation of generations). In particular it seems to be different from the generation, or generations, to which such writers as Unamuno and Ortega might be said to belong. Unamuno and Ortega – perhaps not entirely unjustifiably – as well as other writers – less justifiably – promoted themselves as "literary stars", as "personalities". On the other hand, it seems to be our characteristic to be as modest as an intellectual can be, and, at any rate, to shun the idea of becoming "public figures". This "modesty" is not, or is not entirely, a personal virtue – assuming, of course, that modesty is a virtue; it is rather a result of the historical circumstances in which we have lived. We share this characteristic with a number of European intellectuals of the same (or similar) generation, and in that sense we are more "Europeans" than all the staunch Spanish "Europeanizers" of the past. We are not "personalizable", in the sense of not becoming, or even wishing to become, "great personalities".

Professor Aranguren has outlined a number of features of the Spanish literary Generation of 1936. He has mentioned, among others, one which is related to what I have just said : the fact of "being in a situation" (and a rather uneasy one, for that matter), of standing at a crossroads, with a great deal of self-discontent which leads us to look at our own work with a critical eye. Now, this happens to be true for some of the members of what I may call "our generation", but not necessarily true, or less obviously true, for other members of the same generation. It may be said that "exceptions prove the rule", but in literary, or intellectual, history exceptions should not be easily dismissed. Some members of the Generation of 1936 (in the logical sense of "some", namely, "at least one") are considerably less self-critical and less "personality-minded" than the majority are.

There is a further point. In some of the members of the Generation of 1936 we can detect a certain impatience with, and distrust of, rhetoric – in the pejorative sense of the word. In any case, there are at least two members of the same generation who are plainly anti-rhetorical : Professor Aranguren and myself. I am not sure, however, that everyone shares this feature; Laín Entralgo certainly does not. Now, I am not saying thereby that Laín Entralgo is guilty of anything. To be sure, he is not guilty of being arrogant; quite to the contrary, he is one of the most sincerely modest and kindest persons I have ever encountered. His "rhetorical" propensities are, in fact, the consequence of a very deep intellectual modesty, and also the result of his extreme generosity, and they have nothing to do with the rhetorics of the nineteenth century or of the beginnings of the twentieth century. All things considered, however, the fact remains that his intellectual "style" is quite different from others, for instance from Aranguren's. In general, then, differences as well as similarities should be pointed out when examining the work of the members of the Generation of 1936. Thus far, we have been intent on emphasizing affinities. It is desirable that differences be not left out of the picture, and I assume that in the less general type of talk in which, for professional reasons, Professor Aranguren and myself have indulged, the participants in this colloquium will help us to ascertain such differences. At this point, I suddenly remember that this is a colloquium and, therefore, should be a dialogue, and I am ashamed that my monologue has lasted more than even monologues should.

On Rhetoric and Other Matters*

JOSE LUIS ARANGUREN

The first thing I have to say is that I feel very ashamed since Professor Ferrater-Mora, with great kindness, said that he and I, among the essayists, were the least rhetorical. I now feel, compared with the way in which he just spoke, atrociously rhetorical for the way I spoke earlier. Therefore I will try to change my *tone* in order to get in *tune* with him.

I believe that Professor Ferrater-Mora and I agree on at least one thing (surely on many others, too), and it is that we do not emphasize, from let us say a philosophical point of view – which is not incompatible with what Professor Durán said – the primacy of the concept "generation", but rather, that of reality. For if we put the concept of "generation" first and foremost, we construct a kind of idealism, in the philosophical sense, an idealism of generations. With this concept of idealism, what we would do, would be to organize the whole of reality; in the same way, one might say that linguistic philosophy is an idealisation of language, starting from language.

It seems, then, that Professor Ferrater-Mora and I agree that what is of truly primary importance is reality itself and particularly when it is a matter of great impact, as in the case of the War of 1898, the disaster of 1899, which also had its positive side; I do not refer exclusively now to the reaction, the regeneration, etc., but also – I believe one should always be a little Marxist, not too much, but a little – to the great importance it had for the economic feasibility of an intellectual life, the enormous repatriation of capital that occurred as a consequence of the loss of Cuba and the Philippines. This available capital gave rise to the entire printing industry that has played such an important part and without which – why should we deceive ourselves? – Ortega would not have played anything like the great role he has in the contemporary history of ideas, of literature and as a publisher, etc. . . . So, I repeat, and this in my judgment is not incompatible with a pragmatic view of the concept "generation" – as Professor Durán suggested very well – I am not much in favor of starting from the concept of "generation" and forcing reality to adjust to our predetermined pigeon-hole. This apart, such pigeon-holing and chronological limits lead to very amusing conceptions and in which one notices the effort to be the head of a generation.

*Originally published in *Symposium* XXII (1968); translated by Constance Sullivan.

I doubt that either Professor Ferrater-Mora or I have fallen into that temptation, and besides, as far as I am concerned, I would have no right at all, under penalty of pride, to do so. But I remember – if I may be permitted, since we have renounced all rhetorical tones – that once Marías, the master *par excellence* among us in matters of generations, spoke to me about whether Professor Laín, he and I belonged or not to the same generation. According to Marías, Laín evidently did not belong to our generation. To accept this would explain Laín's (excellent) rhetoric to which Professor Ferrater-Mora referred earlier, because he would not belong to our generation. Here is Marías' reasoning : before he knew me well, he said, he thought that the Generation of 1936 (or whatever one wants to call it; he, naturally, probably called it something else, because he prefers designations according to the year of birth rather than to the year of literary presence) began exactly in 1910 and with those born in 1910. Professor Laín was born in 1908 and I in 1909, but – at least at that time – Marías was willing to put it back one year. Which is, I remind you, fabulous (no one among you, naturally, would do this, because you're all young, but many women subtract years) : with a few exceptions, one can't subtract fifteen years at one stroke. However, thanks to this slight change, it happened. Since to pass from one generation to another involves subtracting nothing less than fifteen years all at once, Marías made me fifteen years younger, which I could have used. I hope he is still willing to make me the same concession. Thus you can see to what extent this is all a convenience. I think that in any case, we are all very modest, and Marías is, too, but a bit less so than we are. I believe, then, that what Marías was subconsciously leaning toward at that time was : since Laín appeared to be a very important figure, well, let him be important, but in another generation, where he could fight out the leadership spot with those of the "dictatorship" and those of the "Generation of 1927" or "of 1925" or "of 1923", or whatever you want to call it. Marías, on the other hand, would thus appear as the unmistakeable head of his generation. So you see that the concept of "generation" thus applied serves precisely the purpose one wants it to serve. I therefore prefer an operative, pragmatic use of it, not with reference to oneself but to others. If one is unfortunate or lucky enough to belong to the Generation of 1936, he should act as though he did not, when reflecting on it.

Professor Ferrater-Mora, in that game of paradoxes he presented, said that if the War had not occurred there would not have been a "Generation of 1936" and, obviously, the "Generation of 1936" would have been much like the "Generation of the Dictatorship". I would say that the fact is, as Professor Durán said in recalling Marx's statement "they made our history for us", the War had to happen. Of course, it's very easy to say that after the fact, and add that a historian is a prophet in reverse and always accurate. The difficulty lies in accurate prediction. In any case, using the sociologist Merton's idea of "the self-fulfilling prophecy", we could say that we have here a prophecy that had to fulfill itself, but, although those on both sides were absolutely committed to confrontation, perhaps they might not have confronted each other in such a bloody way. Suppose the war had ended quickly; then what happened in 1936 would have seemed more like the events of 1898. But, in any case, it seems that it was inevitable and it is therefore too idealistic to suppose that it might not have happened. I think Professor Ferrater-Mora will pardon me, with his usual willingness to do so.

He pointed out another characteristic, that our style – or, rather, since I said that we were not to include ourselves, Ferrater-Mora's style – is very European and that as a result, one cannot comprehend the generation without situating it in that European context. I believe that to be absolutely correct. Naturally, one can say that Ortega was very European, or at least a great Europeanizer. But Ortega's Europeanism referred to himself, and was full of his conviction that he was the leader of his generation. This, by the way, I don't deny. We, on the other hand, have renounced almost without exception any pretentions to leadership. It seems to be characteristic of the generation that none of us feels he is a "sacred monster"; we are absolutely sure that we are not "sacred monsters". This is not modesty, but our consciousness or, if you will, conscience, in the moral sense or whatever other sense, since one probably should not separate conscience from awareness. However that may be, it seems to me that we have another feeling about ourselves that is much more in tune with what is happening today in philosophy all over the world. Today there is no longer a Heidegger, nor a Jaspers, nor even a Wittgenstein. No one aspires to such important positions : men write philosophy, some better than others – very well, like Ferrater-Mora, very poorly, like me – but no one aspires in the field of philosophy to that kind of "leadership" that was characteristic of that other generation.

To conclude, and in reference to rhetoric, aside from the explanation I suggested earlier using Marías' delimitation, perhaps one might refer here to the idea that José María Valverde outlined. That is, that although we may belong to the same generation, there has been a confrontation, the two generations, or the two parts of the generation, have been divided. Probably Falangism, which, like all movements of its type, is by nature very rhetorical, has had to leave its stylistic imprint, even when one stops being a Falangist. Professor Ferrater-Mora cited Laín Entralgo's case, but Ridruejo's is typical, too. Without any reflection on their merit, they are, as he recognized, two very rhetorical persons, in the excellent sense of the word. And I am willing to admit, indeed, I do admit, that one of my greatest defects is that I do not have the command of the spoken word that a good rhetorician always has. But perhaps it behoves us to bear in mind that one can give up ideas much more easily than one can divest oneself of that rhetorical repertory of gestures, reflexes, attitudes, and handling of words, and that as a result, it is normal for the latter to remain when the former have disappeared.

I do not know if I have succeeded, although without his wit, in getting a bit in tune with Professor Ferrater-Mora, and if therefore I may be excused for my earlier rhetoric. If not, I ask your forgiveness.

The University of California, Santa Barbara

On the Chronology of the Generation of 1936*

MANUEL DURAN

There must be a totally logical and plausible way to demonstrate the existence of the Generation of 1936. It is almost a syllogism. Or perhaps an ontological argument. I am a professor; professors concern themselves with serious, valid things that exist; I concern myself with the Generation of 1936, and therefore, that generation exists.

I think that there is, to some degree, an urgent need to clarify certain problems that are in part problems of dates, of relationships between these generations. With each attempt at clarification, we are made uncomfortable by the fact that *these generations do not fit in a symmetrical and orderly fashion* into the historical process. One of the simplest ways to solve the problem would be, as someone has indicated, simply to turn our backs on it, abandon it, or in other words, resolve that we will not bother any longer with generations. This is in effect what had often been done in the past and is still done today when, for example, one writes a book on nineteenth-century literature. Seldom is an analysis made by generations. It is done sometimes, but in many other cases these decades are divided into larger periods, romantic and realistic. And there the question ends.

In a way, the twentieth century has made our analysis more difficult, because it has given us a torrent, an avalanche of movements that are jammed together, complicating matters for each other, and suddenly the "—isms" have failed us, in part because of their very excessive abundance. Exhausted by this multiplicity of movements that we have not been able to fit in, that we have not been able to put in order, we have retreated to a semi-biological series of divisions. And that is where those of us who are thinking of the totality of 20th century literature have, in a way, complicated it for ourselves instead of solving the problem. Obviously, our duty is to fight against chaos. But if we fight against chaos in too strict a manner we run the risk of "throwing the baby out with the bathwater". In other words, of forcing literature into molds to the point where the movement of history, the evolution of styles and, above all, the attention that each individual work merits, become indistinct, are lost or blotted out. Each time

*Originally published in *Symposium* XXII (1968); translated by Constance Sullivan.

we lose sight of the authors and force them totally into an iron framework, into a "literary corset", we betray our attitude as historians or critics of literature.

Nevertheless, in this instance we cannot do without generations. We cannot function clearly without them and are thus condemned to flail about in this sea of generations and also to explain in one way or another how it is that generations do not succeed one another in a rhythmic, ordered way, like waves that hit the shore, and how it is that we have the feeling that *they are beginning to arrive ever more quickly.* Is history itself adopting a quicker rhythm? Are we changing more rapidly? To be sure, biology has not changed to that extent. If we have a generation in 1898 and we assume another in 1927, we immediately are faced with a problem of equilibrium, of rhythms, of geometric vision. Something is not working here. In simple terms, we see that the Generation of 1936 is very close to that of 1927, while on the other hand, there is a greater distance between those of 1898 and 1927. Two solutions are possible : to postulate a generation between 1898 and 1927, or assume that the Generation of 1936 is, in itself, very special. I would advocate, possibly, the second solution.

Marx said that man makes his own history, not the history he wants, but the one he can make. Obviously, the people who were beginning to think and write in 1936 did not make the history they wanted; history exploded in their midst, in their hands, like a bomb. Therefore I think that one can say that *the Generation of 1936 includes all the writers who were profoundly and critically wounded by history,* by the history of those years and the history of the years immediately following the Civil War. In some cases we note that some men do not seem to have been so seriously wounded by history and we then have the impression that they do not form part of this Generation of 1936 except from a biological point of view. In other cases, there are people who were already mature but who nevertheless felt the flow and reacted to it in such a way that they showed themselves to be young – because when one still has enough mental elasticity to react it is because one is young – and they then converted that wound into the very axis of their existence as men and as writers. We find *exceptions,* in people who seem too old in years to belong to the Generation of 1936, but whom, however, we cannot exclude when we think of this generation.

So here we are, faced with a special kind of chaos, numerous paradoxes, and a very fluid situation. We have been partly successful in our endeavour to put history in order, but we have created new problems. If these problems are useful in understanding a series of concrete literary works, then the idea of the Generation of 1936 is not only valid but indispensable. If these problems, instead of clarifying the situation and permitting us a deeper penetration into the work of the writers in this group, do not help us to see clearly into the work, then I would say that the generational concept has not functioned in this case.

Therefore I would propose a *pragmatic and provisional acceptance* of the idea of the Generation of 1936. Let us try out this idea; see what happens, see how it works. If it works, we will accept it. This idea has worked in the case of the Generation of 1898. I think that grouping these writers this way turns out to be an almost indispensable concept, and each time the idea of the Generation of 1898 has been attacked the attack has failed and the idea of that Generation has remained almost intact. In the case of 1927 (or 1925 or 1928, it doesn't much matter) the idea of this generation has made headway and has been generally quite fruitful. I think that in the case of the Generation of 1936 it may also be fruitful, but it is up to us to prove it. That is, we shall not automatically start from this idea, but we will apply it simply as a provisional idea and see what happens. I think it will be useful, but I am not convinced that it will automatically serve to clarify everything and I am not even sure that we can arrive at fully-detailed results without making, as Ferrater-Mora said, a differentiation of lines, which go in different directions, among the groups that have been mentioned with respect to this generation. In short, I say simply that we should accept the existence of a Generation of 1936 provisionally and pragmatically.

Yale University

The Generation of 1936:
One Writer's Plea for Remembering*

ILDEFONSO-MANUEL GIL

I am not interested in applying any method of defining literary generations to the much discussed Generation of 1936. If it is an historical-literary reality, I am part of it. And if it does not exist, and if there can only be generations for the convenience of literary historians, then I am a writer who wanders alone, without a place of refuge.

Due to my position within this reality, I have evaded the issue in my work as a scholar and critic. I could not pass judgment on that generation which would be free of burdensome prejudices and accusations. The history of contemporary Spanish literature is being written on the basis of factions in some cases, and personal friendships in others. To enter the fray for the purpose of dispelling intrigues can only be done from without, from a standpoint impossible for one who directly and indirectly must figure both as judge and participant.

If the Generation of 1936 exists, I belong to it. For that reason I must outline the problems involved not from the broad perspective of the historian or the critic, but by limiting the discussion to my own immediate experiences. This is what I propose to do on the occasion of this symposium, taking the liberty of not even bothering to organize my ideas, memories and impressions.

I cannot avoid an inner annoyance when I think that the name of my literary generation must be tied to the year in which the progress of Spain toward a system of political liberty and dignity was interrupted. What is worse, to the year in which open season on man was declared and thousands of Spaniards were victimized, while other thousands let loose the murderer they carried crouched in the depths of their being.

I have a conciliatory spirit; I love peace; I still believe, in spite of so many national and world-wide historical events, in the dignity of man. But my love of peace and my eagerness for conciliation exclude the submissive and degrading indifference that accepts past events and the forgetfulness of what happened in Spain beginning with July of 1936. When I read that "the war, happily, is far away – although not as far as some of us would like, confronted with reactionaries and madmen", I feel something similar to the urge to vomit on the page just read.

*Originally published in *Symposium* XXII (1968); translated by Constance Sullivan.

I am a writer of the generation which was most terribly marked by the Civil War, the one that has sensed most in its own destiny the problem of Spain. For us that problem has been not merely food for thought, an emotional and intellectual concern; it has also meant prison, persecution, and – in the most painful cases – death. The whole problem of Spain, with all its antecedents and consequences, exploded during those bloody days. For that reason we know that its solution must be based on the terrible reality of 1936–1939, on a war that is not distant, that should never be allowed to disappear into time, because it is the most difficult and most potentially fruitful lesson we Spaniards ever received.

The greatest justification of our lives is to make it impossible for anything like it to happen again, and that is not achieved by forgetting, but by obsessive remembering. We must return again and again to a detailed and profound examination of those events, because we must make known what should never be repeated.

Without doubt, 1936 is a decisive year in the history of our literary generation and it is logical that those who have affirmed its existence did not hesitate when giving it that name. The fact that the name is justified does not free me from my personal annoyance.

I ought to repeat here that I am writing freely and "letting myself go" impelled by the strictest sincerity, that I speak as a writer of the generation and with no intention of avoiding the invalidation of this statement's objectivity by my excessive use of the first person. Such objectivity, in the improbable instance that I were to achieve it or manage to simulate it, would serve no purpose, for with it I would betray my personal condition and my condition as a writer : my participation in these sessions is as a member of the Generation of 1936. When I was invited as such, I was given *carte blanche* to confront the topic somewhat autobiographically.

I here just said that the name is one that I don't like, however valid the reasons on which it is based. When people began to talk of that generation, when it became evident that among very different writers there existed strong ties that authenticated the collective entity, I would have preferred that we had been baptized with another name : Generation of 1931. If the designation was to originate in an historical event, the dates of publication of our first works did not matter as much as the level of receptivity to the historical happening.

In all the history of Spain I find no page with more dignity, patriotism, joy and hope than April 14, 1931. Those of us who then were beginning to write, or were thinking of beginning to write, that is, with decided literary vocation, received the influence of all that greatness in the decisive moment in which our literary personalities were formed. We had been developing in the political struggles against the dictatorship, and the radiant happiness of April 14 illuminated even the deepest folds of our consciousness. Whatever our later ideological evolutions were, and whether we like it or not, what really lies in our hearts is nostalgia for those days.

The year 1936 was almost the year of our destruction (there are those who speak of that same generation as "the destroyed generation"); certainly it was the year of our temporary collapse. While the writers of previous generations saved something, even in the worse of cases, we had lost everything. But just as in the presence of the tragic misfortune of Spain we were sustained by the assurance that tyranny can slow up but not block definitively the progress of a people toward their liberty, we were sustained in the presence of our fate as "crushed" writers by the firmness of our vocation and the assurance that a justifying mission was planned for us by those same adverse events.

Am I writing about politics or about literature? I honestly believe that I am specifying the real meaning of our generation, starting from its true common background.

Our participation in the events of 1930 and 1931 removed us from the close guidance of the Generation of 1927 and led us toward Unamuno, Antonio Machado and Ortega. And it moved us away from the brilliant and joyful temptation of the poetic and literary game, to bring us nearer to the integrity of flesh-and-bone man. United with him in a common cause, we tried to tell the truth; responsible to our accepted condition as writers, we tried to tell it in the best possible way.

While owing a great deal to the writers of the Generation of 1927, we were determined to travel other roads. We had begun to travel them when the catastrophe broke out.

What happened in 1936, and has persisted to the present day, although it is now in evident decline, was the event that distorted our literary generation. The fact that one speaks of the "destroyed generation" is clear recognition of our existence and that although we were not destroyed, we were at least threatened with destruction. A crushing blow from which all the things we had in common gradually began to emerge.

With few exceptions, the writers of the Generation of 1936, even those who had fought or were still fighting in the ranks of the victors, were dedicated to the preservation of cultural values that were threatened or condemned. We succeeded in obstructing the completion of the ideological vacuum that the Franco regime attempted to create; we made names like Unamuno, Antonio Machado, Ortega, García Lorca, Miguel Hernández, as well as those of other writers then in exile, emerge from the depths of official condemnation to the point where the young were aware of them. On the parched land we dropped again the seeds of liberty. And, at the same time, those of coexistence. We knew that the harvest was so far in the future that it would be very unlikely that we ourselves would ever participate in it. But we were sure that this was our duty.

It should be noted that in all the attempts to open cultural doors there were always men of the Generation of 1936 in the front lines and that – again with a few exceptions – a shadow of silence was cast over these men.

In the post-war years there was much talk of the two Spains, the victor and the one in exile. But history will have to speak of a third Spain : the silent one. That is, the Spain that had been reduced to silence and had to come out of it by dint of abnegation and not without leaving behind shreds of dignity in exchange for the ability to fulfill its mission of cultural continuity and the opening of paths to coexistence.

That was the task of the early years of the post-war period, an obscure job of groundwork without which the younger writers – who since then have not wanted, or not known how, to recognize what they owed to the "destroyed generation" – could not have begun to work in the open.

While that was our task in those difficult years, our generational mission could not end there. We, the writers of the Generation of 1936, will justify ourselves if we are true to our condition as special witnesses, as well as to our will to conciliate : coexistence in dignity and liberty.

We must speak and write a great deal about that ominous Civil War. Precisely because we do not want to see it repeated, we should make sure that its terrible lesson is not forgotten. We are not responsible for 1936, nor are we its heirs; we have suffered its consequences more than most. But we are not concerned for our personal destiny but rather for the destiny of each Spaniard. When, for example, our poetry became deeply involved in childhood memories, in the exaltation of family life, we were pointing out the only human values that were left standing firm. Instead of applying methodical doubt, we applied methodical faith : believing and making others believe in some basic values upon which one could later effect, step by step, the reconstruction of a Spaniard not annihilated by shame, nor brainwashed by official propaganda.

I think that all of us who are writers of the Generation of 1936 are determined to write facing the truth, beyond hatred and within justice. The Civil War, as the theme of our works, has scarcely begun its journey.

Brooklyn College of the City University of New York

42

III

A GENERATION OF POETS

Introduction

The next two sections deal with the least controversial area concerning the writers of 1936, namely the poetry of the thirties and forties. The articles collected in sections III and IV, while varying considerably in scope and subject, are not intended to present a comprehensive account of all the poets of the group. The essays, taken together, nonetheless afford a fairly penetrating and representative analysis of the most critical problems involving the general literary trends or the work of an individual poet.

The first two papers, each in their own way, are good introductions to the first wave of poets (described briefly in our General Introduction), and both make references to an additional element common to many of these poets : a renewed religious consciousness which establishes links with a longstanding tradition of Spanish poetry and which carries over into a considerable quantity of post-war verse. (A fairly complete collection of such poetry can be seen in *Poesía religiosa,* ed. Leopoldo de Luis [Madrid and Barcelona, 1969].) The last essay of section III documents the changes in attitudes which take place during the middle thirties in the transition from one esthetic to another, and the intervening companion pieces are devoted to Miguel Hernández and Leopoldo Panero, two members of the Generation whose work was cut short by death.

In section IV, the first paper deals comprehensively with the social attitudes expressed in the poetry that emerges as a response to the hardships of the post-war conditions, while the remaining essay analyzes a key poem of Blas de Otero. As the most vigorous new poet of the forties, the latter writer forms a bridge between the Civil War generation and the younger poets of the later forties and fifties who contributed to the mainstream of Spanish verse.

The Generation of 1936, Almost from Within*

JOSE MARIA VALVERDE

I confess that when I received the very kind invitation to come here, I hesitated for several days, because my ties to this generation (of close friendship with some and of acquaintance with all of its members who have been in Madrid) deprive me of the perspective and objectivity which are necessary if one is to undertake a task which is the province of the literary historian. This closeness may possibly give to my remarks the interest of a first-hand testimony, but at the same time it is a liability. For example, I fear that if I have never considered Miguel Hernández as a member of this generation, but rather as the last member of the preceding one, it may be simply due to the fact that I never met him in person. Turning to another aspect, if I have always – and much more of late – regarded José Luis Aranguren as a member of my own generation (I don't know yet what chronological tag it will carry), it is possible that I have been influenced also by what he implied in his preceding comments : that for more than twenty years, about half my life, he has been my closest friend. But, in any case, I will talk of this group, as I have known it.

I must begin by confessing a certain distaste for the use of the concept of generation, because it seems to me to be a Hegelian device to devalue what each individual has and what each literary work has, and strip them of their merit by reducing everything to an abstraction fit for insertion into History. But at the same time it is inevitable that we professors should speak of generations, since curricula are made up that way and because books need indices, either with or by generations. Since this is unavoidable, then, I wish to point out that, in my opinion, there is a sharp contrast between the historical entry this generation has had and that of its predecessor. I am going to indicate this very rapidly because, among other things, I am speaking when this series of papers should already be concluded. This forces me to summarize my notes rather than read them.

The preceding generation, the so-called Generation of 1927, had various phases, each with a marvellous impact and an extraordinary opportunity in historical development. During the "roaring 20's" that generation carried the avant-garde to an extreme; it was the moment that one of the members of the

*Originally published in *Symposium* XXII (1968); translated by Constance Sullivan.

45

group, María Zambrano, has called "the festival of Spanish poetry". But it also anticipated the great spiritual crisis to come. Consider, for instance, that Alberti wrote *Sobre los ángeles* two years before the famous Wall Street "crash". After that great crisis, in the early 30's, this generation entered into a period of authentic recognition of human anguish, the most profound human problems, giving primary importance to the socio-political element which was, and rightly so, the dominant factor. Perhaps, like the earlier phase, this new relation to the march of history may have given added historical resonance to the group's undoubted merit. But successes in literature do not come cheaply, and when history proceeds in accord with someone, and is used by him as a loudspeaker, there is always the danger that a negative phase will then arrive, in which that "being in tune" will end in tragedy. Thus it was with that generation : after 1936 it saw itself – almost all its members – being carried off to death or exile. These things (you might say) would also serve as sounding-board or loudspeaker, but they undoubtedly constitute a tragedy. That has not exactly been the destiny of the Generation of 1936. This group, when the moment of the Spanish Civil War arrived, was still slightly immature in its figures and books and, nevertheless, obliged to accept a commitment that in some cases depended not on a political choice but simply on geography. There have been, then, two Generations of 1936, the exiles and those who were not : and we must note well those who were not, because until now we have been hearing about those who left, when it may be that the deepest tragedy has been that of those who remained. Above all I wish to point out the case of some who, in principle, supported the political regime that triumphed and even wore the blue shirt. Well then, what has become of them? How have they developed? José Luis Aranguren has alluded already to the process of rectification of some of them and has pointed out this process, this heroic attempt they made to restore some values, to "liberalize", although the word these days is somewhat discredited. I have to speak, inevitably, from my own personal and autobiographical point of view. I remember, in the barren Madrid of the years 1941 and 1942, when the review *Escorial* appeared. I was at that time a boy, but a boy enamoured of poetry, and I found that in the review there was an attempt, in the first place, to gather together names that were not in positions of authority, like that of Menéndez Pidal, for example, a name relatively innocuous today, but whose appearance in a magazine that carried official sanction was almost a scandal. It was not for nothing that, some years later, the organizers of that initiative, Ridruejo and Laín Entralgo, were violently expelled from their positions. But, turning to poetry, which was my favorite subject then, as it has been ever since, I found there poets who had new personalities. At first glance, those poets sounded modern to me, that is, I saw in them a unity with those other poets of the preceding generation (that of 1927) who sometimes almost obsessed me by their "avant-garde" enthusiasm, as if it were a sport. These were similar; they inherited, as it were, the same *innovating* stylistic tone. But there was in them a different spiritual position, a position we might indicate vaguely as more or less stemming from Catholicism, an Unamunesque Catholicism, profound, new, and which we were to see later end in a moment of fruitful crisis. (This crisis was not going to harm those poets as much as it was to harm Aranguren, who for some years was on the brink of excommunication,

46

although after the Second Vatican Council he has become almost a Venerable of the Church.) These poets, then, presented something very important for me, a kind of synthesis of the modern, the new, with the Generation of 1898 and the traditional, since the Golden Age could also be seen in them (and, I add in passing, certainly more of the Baroque than of the Renaissance). All this was tied, as I said, to a spiritual position that, as I have indicated in the case of Aranguren, would be more clearly manifest in intellectuals than in poets.

It is difficult to tell you what my relationship with these poets – Leopoldo Panero, Rosales, Vivanco – has been. First of all I am going to speak of Panero, but rapidly, briefly, and with reticence. There is a tragedy in Panero's life that I cannot speak of here at length. It has been a painful paradox to think that the man who around 1945 or 1946 was considered, in my sphere, the "Red" *par excellence,* was to pass through a phase during which he was almost the official poet. Naturally, Panero was never interested in politics, or anything like that; and what is typical of the position of these poets is that their eventual approximation to the regime won them absolutely no material benefit nor personal prosperity. Panero (I will deal simply with the story that I cannot develop now), perhaps on a trip to Latin American countries, on a journey of frustration and failure, reached a state of crisis that prompted him to write an unhappy book, addressed to Neruda, that caused him difficulty with the young, who at that time were beginning to disagree emphatically with the Spanish regime. Perhaps this led to an internal nervousness that may have contributed to his death : in Panero's death, a premature death, there is a psychological and intimate element that we cannot ignore. So for Panero, I repeat, politics was nothing more than an external hazard; what was profound in him was his tragedy as a poet. He had let a lot of time go by; for too many years he had not faced that social aspect of poetry that is publication, the launching of a book that automatically becomes a strange being, and suddenly, very tardily, he published a book (and what is more, at a time when other books of his poetical group appeared and had greater success). This, perhaps, left him slightly disconcerted regarding his own work as a poet. His major work, "La estancia vacía", which was to be a great poem of intimate nature, a tale of life in the romantic Wordsworthian sense, was interrupted, not for lack of time (he wrote thousands of lines) but because he had lost the right moment for this experience when a poet faces himself in time, objectivized in a printed and bound form.

I think also of the case of Luis Rosales, not the tragedy, but the abnegation of Luis Rosales who, after having had the opportunity to be someone officially very important in Spain, elegantly declined it all – a university chair, economic ease – and, living from some badly paid odd jobs, took refuge in the Manuscript Room of the National Library to compile his immense file on baroque poetry that afterwards was of no practical use to him. I recall that there were years when Luis Rosales was stuck away in his corner, not seeing anyone, and I used to go to see him. Like a blind man's guide, I took him out a little, introducing him to people, above all to some poets who were then arriving from Latin America and who became very important for me and also for him. These poets, creating for us an environment of high lyric temperature, of the creative word, with those nights of reading poetry for eight or ten hours at a stretch put him back into creative activity. That was when he again began to be productive and he published "La casa encendida". If there were time enough at this meeting I would like you to hear this poem. (I have it here on tape, in an exciting reading organized for the students at the University of Barcelona, who saw with surprise that the poet they had already wiped from their list was one of the really alive poets in Spain.) That was almost twenty years ago. Rosales then wrote his "Rimas", in which there was a small echo of the great force of that earlier poem. Since then he has become a more and more marginal figure, as also in the political sphere.

I am going to speak very briefly of Vivanco. Aside from the fact that I married into his family, there is a more significant circumstance for the purposes of literary exposition. I believe that Vivanco is still in the fullness of his work, that precisely now he is at the zenith of his work. He has shown a wise, and at times a cruel, astuteness, holding himself in reserve, standing dauntless, implacable in his poetic position as a contemplator of the things of the world – not in an inhuman way although I admit that at first it seemed so to me. Now I realise that Vivanco's contemplative objectivity was and should be the prelude to a possible observation of human beings around him, because it was more than anything a search for man's internal equilibrium, his moral foundations, and only from that point is it possible for poetry to assume a truly social character, as today, with good reason, everybody tries to achieve.

The hour and the fact that we are behind schedule suggests that I should finish : the "round table" discussion will come later. I have spoken only of these poets, and I have not spoken of the intellectuals. For instance, I should have talked about Laín Entralgo, whom I met shortly after the appearance of the review *Escorial* and who, precisely from that point, from an initial attitude of somewhat naive Falangism, came out with an open attitude of generosity that not only has given him a solid latent power in the future of Spain, but which has helped some of us to play a larger part in national life than perhaps we would have otherwise – a role dissenting, to be exact, from that which he initially represented.

I could have spoken also of Ridruejo : Ridruejo, the poet who was totalitarian in a way that one might say was almost moving, in an intense, thrusting, sportive way, and who for that very reason today applies that same energy – and I am afraid, that same naivete – to the purpose of a democratic movement in Spain. But I believe it is best to end my remarks here, not to consume more time and simply to leave an opening so that later, in the "round table" discussion, you may ask me what you wish, completing this rapid, summarized talk.

Trent University, Canada

The Poetry of the Generation of 1936[1]

E. INMAN FOX

Because of the wealth, in both quantity and quality, of the Spanish lyric in the twentieth century and the lack of any unbiased and sensible treatment – despite the numerous books and articles on the subject – of the modes and modulations of its historical development, the critic is continually forced to reinterpret, or to interpret seriously for the first time, individual poets and even groups of them. If his original purpose is to clarify a moment in the history of poetic expression with the vague hope of contributing to a general understanding, more often than not he finds a new and refreshing individual poetic expression which is worth communicating to his readers.

In the case at hand, many present-day critics have accepted the existence, and even the importance, of a generation of poets that first appeared in print in 1935 and 1936[2], but apart from their contemporaries few have bothered to read their poetry with any discernment.[3] In these years several books that disregarded to some extent the poetic norms of the day were published by poets all in their twenties, but who were so well endowed that they had immediate

[1]This essay derives from a lecture given at the Universities of Edinburgh, Nottingham, Cambridge and London in the British Isles, and Wesleyan University in Middletown, Connecticut.

[2]The term "Generation of 1936" was first coined by Professor Homero Serís. It has since been talked of, in a very general sense, as a generation of writers whose youthful intellectual development was affected in one way or another by the Civil War. Others have used the grouping simply as a way to talk about the Spanish writers born between 1909 and 1915. It has always been a rather artificial concept of literary history – perhaps inspired in the ever-increasing number of generations in Contemporary Spanish Literature: those of 1898, 1914 and 1927 – and is rejected by most critics. However, one can contribute to the understanding of the history of contemporary poetry by studying the poets of this generation as a group. From this point of view, the July–August 1965 issue of *Insula* provides valuable information.

[3]Although in fragmented fashion, the excellent book of Charles David Ley, *Spanish Poetry since 1939* (The Catholic University of America Press, 1962), contributes invaluably to our understanding of these poets with his bibliographical information, his studies of the many poetry reviews and the publication of interviews with the poets themselves. I refer the reader especially to the chapters "Poets who remained in Spain after 1939" and "Neoclassicism". The only serious study of these poets taken as a group is the unpublished doctoral dissertation of Alicia Lockwood, "Cuatro poetas de la Generación de 1936" (Wisconsin, 1966). After an introduction she has individual chapters on Panero, Rosales, Hernández, and Serrano Plaja.

success and evinced admiration from the poets then in vogue, the generation of 1927. These volumes were *Abril* by Luis Rosales, *Cantos de primavera* by Luis Felipe Vivanco, *Sonetos amorosos* by Germán Bleiberg, *La voz cálida* by Ilde-fonso-Manuel Gil, *Destierro infinito* by Serrano Plaja, and *El rayo que no cesa* by Miguel Hernández. At the same time another poet, Leopoldo Panero, was writing in the same style what many consider to be his best poetry : *Versos del Guadarrama.* From the point of view of the literary historian, it is curious that on the heels of the brilliant production of the generation of 1927, still very much in artistic and editorial control, there should emerge a group of young poets with a different and original vision of poetic reality. Although influenced by Lorca, Guillén, Salinas, Cernuda and Aleixandre, as all writers must be by what goes before them, they differentiated themselves by a return to Neo-Classical forms – the sonnet and the hendecasyllable – and they demonstrated a mastery of technique coupled, in many cases, with the complex imagery that all modern poetry has inherited from the symbolists and the surrealists. To be sure, Jiménez, Unamuno, Guillén and others had cultivated the sonnet and other classical forms, and Alberti and Cernuda had written an elegy and an eclogue to Garcilaso, but there existed at the time a general tendency to flee from external form and to write in free verse.

The extraordinary quality of the Facultad de Filosofía y Letras of the University of Madrid bolstered by the activities of the Centro de Estudios Históricos and the Junta para Ampliación de Estudios and the contact that Salinas, Dámaso Alonso, Guillén and the younger poets Rosales and Bleiberg had with these institutions gave a solid and thoroughly academic approach to poetry which was bound to result in a policy of formalist containment with respect to the freedom of expression of the avant garde movements. These poets were well-trained students of the Spanish classics and were imbued with a sense of tradition. There were attempts, of academic origin, to restore the Spanish lyric tradition and incorporate it into modern poetry. We can detect an influence of Lope immediately following José F. Montesinos' edition in Clásicos Caste-llanos of the *Poesía lírica* of Lope in 1925, that of Góngora in the year of the tricentennial, 1927, and the *garcilasismo* in the lyric of 1936. The impact of the Góngora centennial was more critical than creative and its real contribution, in my opinion, was to aid in a better understanding of modern poetry originating with Mallarmé and the symbolists. Or perhaps their ability to re-evaluate Góngora lay in the comprehension of symbolism. It matters little for the two go hand in hand in critical activity. Many imitated Góngora, but besides Gerardo Diego's *Fábula de Equis y Zeda* – written in *octavas* like the *Polifemo* – and Alberti's *Cal y canto,* we see little lasting influence of the *culterano* in the major poets. The *Sonetos amorosos* of Bleiberg and the long eclogues of Rosales (1935) and of Hernández (1936), technically and emotionally inspired in the work of Garcilaso, were, however, to influence much of the poetry written during the Civil War and the first post-war movement, the *garcilasistas.*

Ricardo Gullón has called this group the "generación escindida", or the generation that was cut off, and History was indeed cruel to them. Only a short time after they began to be recognised the Civil War tortured their physical and spiritual lives and scattered them to the winds. Some were Republicans and others were Nationalists and the devastating war rendered asunder the serenity of their production. Miguel Hernández and Germán Bleiberg, for example, spent many years in prison where Hernández was to die; and Luis Rosales, Leopoldo Panero, and Dionisio Ridruejo accommodated themselves so easily to the new regime and supported its ideals so actively that their poetry, in many incidences, suffered the consequences. They all continued to write and *Más allá de las ruinas* (1947) of Bleiberg, *Cancionero y Romancero de ausencias* of Hernández, *La casa encendida* (1949) of Rosales, and *Escrito a cada instante* (1949) of Panero should be on everybody's reading list. Nevertheless, their official lives as poets were cut short. Because of the nature of their later poetry – an insistence on the morality of a not necessarily moral Spain since 1936 – Rosales and Panero have emerged as the most publicized representatives of the group, and this makes them suspect among many intellectuals. Because of the revolutionary tone of many of his poems, a serious consideration of the poetry of Hernández was delayed for many years in Spain. And Bleiberg, although still writing, has developed a general attitude toward poetry as a personal experience to be communicated only to friends or small audiences.[4] In short, with the exception of Hernández, they have been much too forgotten among unbiased readers for reasons wholly extraneous to their work. The criticism on Rosales and Panero – and also the lack of it – has often been motivated by causes foreign to a proper evaluation of poetry; such as political alignment or personal friendship.

The post-war *garcilasista* movement which dominated Spanish poetry from 1940 until 1943 was inspired, as we have stated, in the *garcilasismo* of the poetry of 1936,[5] but neither the poets of the earlier expression nor the spirit of their work participated in this inauthentic and escapist moment of the history of Spanish poetry. The poets of the review *Garcilaso* converted Garcilaso, the symbol of love and death of 1936, into the poet representative of Spanish imperialism resuscitated amidst Franco's regime's preoccupation with Gibraltar, Jamaica, and other lost possessions. It is this mistaken all-inclusive view of the *garcilasista* moment in contemporary Spanish poetry that has most obscured the originality of the poets here treated. My purpose in this article, then, is not to scientifically argue the case of the existence of a "generation" as such – I will use the term throughout as a descriptive convenience – but rather to undertake a brief, and as objective as possible, study of the poetry of those whom I consider to represent best the so-called generation of 1936: Leopoldo Panero, Luis Rosales, Germán Bleiberg and Miguel Hernández.

The themes of their poetry are what may be the only ultimate possible subjects of the lyric : love, death and Nature; the three being almost always inextricably meshed in a pantheistic world where love is the only reality or proof of existence, and death, its absence. It is important to remember that the Spanish poets of the early thirties who wrote in the surrealistic mode had revived these romantic elements and incorporated them into their poetry. The theories of

---

[4]At this writing, we have just learned that Bleiberg is preparing a volume of collected poems for publication by Revista de Occidente under the title *Vigilia*. It will include a prologue in which he explains his silence.

[5]García Nieto, the chief poet of the post-war movement, has said that his poetry was inspired in the *Sonetos amorosos* of Bleiberg, which he constantly read while in a Republican prison (Ley, p. 60).

Nature, Death and Love, overflowing in the irrational poetry of Cernuda, of *La destrucción o el amor* of Aleixandre and of *Residencia en la Tierra* of Neruda, certainly contributed to the revival of Garcilaso. We must also call attention to the importance of the publication by Pedro Salinas of *La voz a ti debida* in 1933. When the poetic world was preoccupied with the industrialization of society, the dream world and automatic writing, he writes a love poem whose diction and vocabulary is sometimes very reminiscent of Garcilaso. The younger poets capitalized on all these elements – the antithetical love theme as well as the surrealistic language – in their refreshing use of Neo-Classical form. In the poetry of Panero, Rosales, Bleiberg and Hernández the themes, as I have said, are similar and there is a likeness of form, imagery, and the use of certain key words. They are, however, a generation of individually important poets. Each one imposes order on his sensations, his emotions – his universe, in short – by the use of varying combinations of form and content, of rhythm and tone; and each achieves an originality which elicits our attention. Because of the impossibility of dispatching a generation of poets in such a limited space, I will concentrate my analytical commentary around a single sonnet written by each immediately before the Civil War (that is in 1935-1936) and will make a general descriptive statement about their later poetry.

The published work of *Leopoldo Panero (1909–1962)* during his early years consisted of surrealistic poems which he later repudiated, but he considered the *Versos del Guadarrama* – the majority of which were written between 1930 and 1936, although they remained unedited until the publication in 1963 of *Poesías* – as true to his mature production and to that of all his generation : that is, a return to essential and existential human emotions expressed in traditional form.[6] This collection starts with a lyrical *romance* reminiscent of the exclamations of Guillén, but immediately shifts into a grave and serene meditation on the landscape expressed in sonnets and long poems in hendecasyllables. Panero, who had been born in Astorga, in the province of León, of which he writes a great deal, was confined to a sanatorium in the Guadarramas during these years because of ill health. He frequented Madrid often where he came into contact with the poets of '27 and those of the younger generation to whom, he tells us, he read his poetry. In these verses he sings sadly of an adolescent love which he sees mirrored in the forbidding mountains covered with snow. It seems that the Guadarramas inspired in him the conviction of the eternity of Nature as against the transitoriness of human passion, which, precisely because of its temporality had to be explained in terms of Creation. Panero's concern with temporality and its reflection in the landscape rings of Machado, but more specifically in these poems we hear echoes of the lines dedicated to the Guadarramas and the Gredos of Enrique de Mesa, an important poet, once esteemed

[6]The only important studies to date that we have on Panero are the essays by Dámaso Alonso, "La poesía arraigada de Leopoldo Panero", in *Poetas españoles contemporáneos* (also included as a prologue to *Poesías* of Panero, Madrid, Ediciones Cultura Hispánica, 1963); and by Luis Felipe Vivanco, "Leopoldo Panero, en su rezo personal cotidiano", *Introducción a la poesía española contemporánea*. Panero's own lecture on poetry, published posthumously in the number of *Cuadernos Hispanoamericanos* (Nos. 187-188, 1965) dedicated to him, is a very important text for the understanding of his poetry.

and now forgotten, who was saturated with Krausism. In Panero, however, we note an interiorization of the landscape, in the manner of Juan Ramón Jiménez, and an humanization which comes in the form of a dialogue between "tú" and "yo". But he never succeeds in merging his personality with that of the landscape and we forever feel that this is the tragic sentiment of Panero : the impossibility of union and a resulting solitude never absent in his poetry. "Estamos solos para siempre. . . ." ("We are alone forever"), ("Sola tú").

I reproduce a typical sonnet :

EL VIEJO ESTIO

La nieve borra el campo blanco y lento,
y el Guadarrama duerme bajo el frío
triste del corazón . . . (¡Igual que el mío,
oh Guadarrama, tu latido siento!)

¡Lejos, hondo, fragante, vasto aliento
dorado del pinar! El viejo estío
– la luna en el canchal, el son del frío –
el alma torna mientras gime el viento.

¡Alegre, alegre luz innumerable
donde empieza la muerte mi desvelo
y la sangre del todo se desnuda!

De amor olvidadizo inolvidable
escucha el corazón brotar del suelo
junto al romero azul el agua muda.

(OLD SUMMER

Snow blurs the slow white field
and the Guadarramas sleep under the sad
coldness of my heart . . . (Just as I do mine,
oh Guadarramas, I feel your heart beat!)

Distant, deep, fragrant, vast, golden
breath of the pine grove! The old Summer
– the moon in the rocky mountains, the sound of the cold –
moves the soul while the wind groans.

Happy, happy innumerable light
where my sleeplessness begins death
and the blood of everything undresses!

My heart listens to the mute water
of forgetful unforgettable love spring forth
from the ground beside the blue rosemary.)

Although the landscape is real in its details, we note that we have something more than a description. The poet has interiorized it : "¡Igual que el mío/ oh Guadarrama, tu latido siento!" ("Just as I do mine, oh Guadarramas, I feel your heart beat!"); "el alma torna mientras gime el viento" ("the soul is moved while the wind groans"); and he has personified it : "duerme", it sleeps, and "vasto aliento", it is breath. The natural sadness of the landscape is identified with a sadness of heart caused by the memory of a love that has forgotten. And, I might add, in Panero the vision of a landscape almost always evokes a loved one. But he is a religious poet and Nature is rarely presented in any other sense than Creation. The heart-landscape-soul fusion, then, becomes an expression of the sublime mystic conception of the universe and life :

> Sobre las rocas, cárdenas, fluyente
> en nitidez y música de esfera,
> parece resonar, tras la ladera,
> la limpia anchura donde Dios se siente.
> > from "Todo en vuelo".

> (Resplendent flow and music of the spheres,
> the clean expanse where God is felt,
> beyond the slope, seems to resound
> against the purple rocks.)

A close examination of this sonnet also reveals two contrasted landscapes separated in time but superimposed one on the other in the poet's imagination : the cold, sad, snowy mountains identified with his state of soul, and the memories of summer, the fragrant pine grove dazzled by the sun with the poet amidst the blooming rosemary listening to the gurgling water. As mentioned before, the tension caused by man's impossibility to achieve more than a moment's contact with the perfection of God's creation is evident throughout Panero. Formally the serenity of the poem is broken by a heavy use of antithesis, a traditional and essential characteristic of all lyrical poetry since Heraclitus, which serves to point up the difficulty of expressing human emotions in words. The antithetical title itself, "el viejo estío", is a brilliant way of telling us that Winter – or even poetry – however sad, melancholic, or filled with memories of things no longer to return it may be, is based on the beauty and passion of Summer. Then there is "olvidadizo inolvidable" ("forgetful unforgettable") and "escucha . . . el agua muda" ("listens to the mute water"), etc. The use of antithesis here though is modern; it does not reflect the classical theory of compensation which says that harmony is found in the juxtaposition of opposites. It seems more an indication of anguish of feeling or frustration of expression which is typical to some extent of all the poets of 1936.

In this sonnet we can observe, then, most of the elements which run throughout the poetic production of Panero. His work is the prime example of the continual statement of transitory man standing before eternal Creation, of the anxiety of the individual in his search for God. It is religious poetry which starts from the basic belief that man must meditate first on his own existence in order to arrive at a confrontation with God or the First Cause. The metaphysical thread and principle theme of *Escrito a cada instante* (1949) is the constant desire to find God through the word and the sense of success and an immediately following failure "a cada instante". In this work Panero poeticizes day-to-day experience as a means to achieve union with God, and his astonishment when faced by concrete reality and light reminds us of Guillén, a poet whose influence is patent in Panero. To poetically establish his connection with God he returns time and time again to a key image : that of the tree rooted deeply in the Spanish soil, whose trunk represents family ties and whose top pushes up toward the sky in search of the Divine Being. The specific inspiration of his later poetry – the comfort of family life, the forever secure and present conjugal love, and the belief in the perfection of the cosmos ordered by God – seems somewhat out of step with the contemporary conception of existence. It has been lamented by everyone that he felt the necessity to poetically defend the Falange in his long poem *Canto personal* (1953), which was an answer to the communist *Canto general* of Pablo Neruda, friend and maestro of all these poets in Madrid during the Republic. However powerful its expression, it reveals the loss of lyric sensibility almost always involved in an intentional defense of a political ideology. In his post-war poetry, although still revealing his mastery of more traditional technique, Panero tends more and more toward the use of free verse in which the metaphor almost entirely disappears. The word becomes all important, but it is never bound by a contradictory epithet, by an antithetical intuition. If there is any of the tension we are accustomed to in modern poetry – in the case of Panero, between loneliness, the condition of man, and presence or salvation by God – it is almost never exploited in a single poem; but must be read into different individual poems which reflect different states of soul of the poet. The feeling that the existential anguish of man is somehow always resolved by the tenderness of matrimony and an ultimate faith in God tends to limit the poetic experience and eliminate a possible ironical contemplation of reality. His poetry does conserve, however, an extraordinary musical quality; and the positive value of Panero's later poetry is the feeling produced that the intimate or poetic reality, no matter how inspired in, or related to, everyday reality, is the only truth.

Luis Rosales, born in 1910 in Granada where he fed on that sensitive group of artists, musicians, and poets that surrounded García Lorca and now a resident of Madrid devoting the majority of his time to the reviews and publications of the Instituto de Cultura Hispánica, is the second poet I shall treat.[7] In his early poetry we do not detect any inspiration derived from a concrete landscape as we do in Panero; it is rather an idealized one in the classical tradition. Here it is worth remembering that he had translated Virgil. In reality, however, there is no landscape as such, but elements of Nature – wind, snow, the sea – that

---

[7] The only study on Rosales with which I am familiar is "El crecimiento del alma en la palabra encendida de Luis Rosales", by Vivanco, *op. cit.* The studies of Vivanco on Panero and Rosales, indeed his whole book, are very curious. He seeks the "palabra poética" – a term now adopted by the whole of the Catholic branch of 1936 – of each poet, but he never manages to define exactly what it is. His interpretations are very rhetorical and he does not seem to be overly sensitive to the mechanism of lyrical expression.

are metaphorically associated and fused with God and the *amada*. In his early poetry Rosales is without question more interesting as a technician in search of a new value of expression to be found in the word, something that he develops with more success than Panero in his later poetry, as we shall see. He writes in a variety of forms and poeticizes a variety of moods.

Abril, published in 1935, was Rosales' first book of poetry and it is indeed a pretentious one for a young poet of 25. It is a long book, carefully divided into parts with epigrams from Herrera, Lope de Vega, San Juan de la Cruz, Garcilaso and García Lorca. It consists of *romances,* elegies, eclogues, sonnets and long poems in hendecasyllables and in free verse. What most interests us now, however, is a collection of ten sonnets, the long religious poem "Misericordia", and an eclogue which is inspired in Garcilaso's *Egloga segunda.* The poet feels abandoned, alone, left only with memories of his "abril perdido" ("lost April"). His verses are filled with the classical *ubi sunt* and *où sont les neiges d'antan.* He suffers from the absence of his loved one, but a naive faith serves as a crutch. He continually appeals to God, insisting that his terrestrial love is no more than a reflection of Love without bounds that fills his soul. He feels he deserves misericordia, not sacrifice, and this is the theme of "Misericordia":

> Tú sabes que yo nunca he negado el presente,
> Y el presente eras Tú, cuando yo te buscaba
> por los rincones de mis ojos heridos,
> por la corriente viva de las aguas, empapadas de cielo,
> y en la nieve.
> ¡A Ti, Señor, Amor sin determinaciones, Presencia sin instante!
> ¡A Ti, Señor!,
> en la nieve absoluta.

> (You know that I have never denied the present,
> and the present was You, when I looked for you
> in the corners of my wounded eyes,
> in the lively current of the rains, soaked by the sky,
> For You, Lord, Love without bounds, Presence without instant!
> and in the snow.
> For You, Lord,
> in the absolute snow.)

The following is a sonnet from *Abril*:

> Bajo el limpio esplendor de la mañana
> en tu adorado asombro estremecido,
> busco los juncos del abril perdido;
> nieve herida eras tú, nieve temprana
>
> tu enamorada soledad humana,
> y ahora, Señor, que por la nieve herido
> con la risa en el labio me has vencido,
> bien sé que la tristeza no es cristiana.

¿No era la voz del trigo mi locura?
Ya estoy solo, Señor – nieve en la cumbre –,
nieve aromada en el temblor de verte,

hombre de llanto y de tiniebla oscura,
que busca en el dolor la mansedumbre,
y esta locura exacta de la muerte.

(Beneath the limpid splendour of the morning
I look for the rushes of the lost April
in your adored trembling astonishment;
wounded snow you were, early snow

your human solitude in love,
and now, Lord, that you have defeated me
wounded by the snow with laughter on my lips,
I know well that sadness is not Christian.

Wasn't my madness the voice of the wheat?
I am now alone, Lord – snow on the peak –
snow made sweet-smelling in the trembling of seeing you,

man of weeping and of dark darkness,
who seeks in pain meekness
and this exact madness of death.)

The antithetical conception of this love poem is characteristic of the poets of 1936. The day is splendid and vibrant, but the poet's state of soul is unaffected. His interior landscape is covered with snow, solitude, and darkness and he can only dream of April : "busco los juncos del abril perdido" ("I look for the rushes of the lost April"). We also come upon key words used by Rosales – *voz* (voice), *dolor* (pain), *llanto* (weeping), *nieve* (snow), *herido* (wounded) – that recur often in his poetry, although without any apparently consistent meaning or metaphorical identification. This, plus the liberty he takes with the sonnet form and Spanish syntax, contributes to a lack of plasticity which draws the reader's attention to the isolated impression produced by words and word combinations. There is, I think, the transference of a legitimate emotion caused by the human error of searching for eternity in physical love. He appeals to God, his only recourse, to soothe his grief and sadness, but seems to think that only upon dying will he cease to feel alone. Nevertheless, the emotion is sublimated by a somewhat contrived technical perfection which doesn't allow form and content to be in harmonious relationship. We feel that some sort of aesthetic design is the ultimate intention (Rosales seems closer to Herrera in these sonnets than to Garcilaso); and the poem itself to some extent resists analysis. The poetic meaning of *nieve*, for example, a word clearly important to the sonnet, is vague : *herida* and *temprana* it is human love and/or purity, in the strict Garcilasan sense (just as *trigo* (wheat) is desire, fecundity, virility in the Renaissance sense); and later it refers

57

to the all encompassing eternal love of God. But certainly they cannot be equated in this poem. In this sonnet, as in most of the poetry of 1936, there is no sustained image that provides structural unity. The total registered impression is one of tone. These poets found their originality of expression not in imagery, but in the juxtaposition of words, of noun and epithet, never seen before. The effect is a highly suggestive language which might, in many instances, shock the unaccustomed reader. Examples in the quoted sonnet are : *nieve herida* (wounded snow), *enamorada soledad* (solitude in love), *locura exacta* (exact madness). I also call your attention to the two combinations *nieve herida,* sufficient in itself, and the similar *por la nieve herido* (by the snow wounded), a stylistic ploy typical of the poets under question – and of the Renaissance poets, I might add – which through changing the object modified (in this case from *nieve* to the tacitly understood *poeta*) still calls to mind the original noun-adjective combination, thereby intensifying the second appearance and unifying the poetic suggestion. I have chosen this poem of Rosales because it is typical of the poet as an influential propagator of the return to Neo-Classicism. He was later to state, however, as a convinced Catholic poet that the cult of Beauty or form *per se* had no place in serious poetry.

Like Panero, Rosales abandons his cult of Garcilaso and writes lyrical poetry with a narrative element. And his later poetry, especially *La casa encendida* (1949), is humanized in the sense that he writes about his childhood, the home and his wife, and the background becomes more concrete. He has said that *vivir* is *el desvivir del corazón* through poetry and the imaginative expression with which he conveys his sentiments is of high lyrical quality. This poetry seems more authentic than that of his neo-classical period; and if, like Panero again, his Catholic constant allows little room for the ups and downs of existence, his poetic imagination is of a much higher order. He is rarely face to face with reality but rather depends on memories; that is, his poetry comes not with the experience itself but in dreaming about it. The dependence on memories and the fact that he poeticizes them as if they were dreams allows him to take advantage of the complexities and the suggestiveness of the language of surrealism. Its modernity belongs to the fact that it is not really surrealistic. He normally uses a surrealistic metaphor to describe something that is common in our daily lives; and he mixes colloquial language with irrational poetry. This marvellous tension between reality and imagination, necessary to all good poetry, is the most important and valuable characteristic of *La casa encendida.* For example, the "house" and its objects are almost always poeticized in terms of the people that are in it, and vice versa. The maid arrives "con aquella alegría de madre con ventanas/que hablaban todas a la vez" ("with that happiness of a mother with windows/ that were all talking at the same time"); she seemed "una lámpara/ vestida con aquel buen aceite tan pálido de la conformidad" ("a lamp/ dressed in that good oil, so pale, of conformity"); and when she sat down, she made "un gesto completamente inútil de pañuelo doblado" ("a completely useless appearance of a folded handkerchief").

La casa encendida is clearly the best poetry of the Catholic group of 1936 which culminates with the publication in 1949 of *Escrito a cada instante, Continuación a la vida* by Luis Felipe Vivanco, and the title mentioned. And it is probably this group of three poets that we could best define as a continuing generation. Of almost exactly the same age, they all started writing love sonnets with religious overtones influenced by Renaissance tradition, were Nationalists during the Civil War, emerged from the war convinced that the future of Spain was secured, were gathered together in the review *Escorial* (1943–1946) and wrote poetry which idealized the proposed values of the new regime. For this reason, they best represent an important poetic attitude that we would do well not to overlook, in spite of our political ideologies.

The work of *Germán Bleiberg* (b. 1915), the youngest poet of the group, has been overshadowed in academic circles by the success of his editorial, critical, and professorial labors.[8] Although his poetry is amply included in anthologies and university publics all over the world have heard him read his unedited poems, his published verses like *Sonetos amorosos, Más allá de las ruinas,* and *La mutua primavera* have not been reprinted and today are not as available to the general reader as might be hoped. Because he developed along different lines from the Catholic group and because his vital anguish, both in expression and attitude, more clearly reflects the psychological state of contemporary man, he seems to be one of the most authentic voices of the group of 1936. In the early years the formal aspects of the poetry of Rosales and Bleiberg were very similar. They were intimate friends and read each other's poetry with sympathy; and there is no question that there existed a mutual influence in their respective manners of expression. The likeness of their poetry, however, is only superficial : where Rosales used classical form in search of poetic technique and ultimately Beauty, the Garcilasan sonnet and hendecasyllable were for Bleiberg a vehicle, trappings, for a more intense preoccupation with existence. And it was an expressive mode that he would abandon in his more mature poetry.

In January of 1936 Bleiberg published in the *Revista de Occidente* a fragment, "Oración a la Muerte", of a long elegy written in tercets and inspired in the poem "Misericordia" of Rosales. The first line, "¿Qué harás de mí, Señor, cuando yo muera?", is the literal translation of the first line of a sonnet by Rilke, a favourite of Bleiberg whose poetry had to leave an impact on his sensibility, as the reader will later understand. Unlike Panero and Rosales, Bleiberg does not, however, associate his earthly love with that of God. Realizing and accepting the limitations of the flesh, he surrenders himself to the pains of human love and feels only the absence of physical love. His poetry then is poetry of existence – and to a great extent existentialist – whose two poles are presence and absence, *amor* and *dolor,* life and death. And it is this compenetration of love and existence which makes him the most profound love poet of his generation.

In the *Sonetos amorosos* (1936), a collection of 17 Petrarchan sonnets, the Arcadian landscape, the natural background which lent harmony to Classical poetry, becomes fragmented into isolated elements which, if ambiguous at times, are nearly always associated with the loved one. It is an idealized landscape – but not an idealized love – whose reality can only be found by the poet by relating it to the characteristics of a woman. She alone is the object of his

---

[8]Bleiberg's poetry has been studied by Charles David Ley, "The Poetry of Germán Bleiberg", *Bulletin of Hispanic Studies, XXVI* (1949); and by the author of this essay, "Germán Bleiberg: Poeta de la existencia", *Symposium* (Summer 1968).

contemplation; and the love that she inspires is poeticized as Nature. Since Bleiberg does not revive the pastoral convention, the verses of Garcilaso that he uses as an epigram to the sonnets, ". . . y aquel sonido/hará parar las aguas del olvido" (". . . and that sound/will stop the waters of oblivion") (*Egloga* III), tell us more perhaps of what he gleaned from the Renaissance poet than longer quotations would. And the fact that they come from the same stanza as Salinas' title *La voz a ti debida* suggests, as the reader will see, a possible comparison of the poetics of the two poets : the constant dialogue between "tú" and "yo", the belief that poetic reality comes only from physical experience, and the necessity to create a "más allá".

These sonnets are lamentations caused by the solitude of the poet, the absence of the lover whom he sees reflected in his imagined landscape. His *llanto* (weeping) is fertile, however, because sad memories can only have their origins in past happiness, and this ambiguity is the stuff from which poetry is made :

Mientras de luz y de esperanza herido
Mi corazón te piensa y te edifica,
Un llanto luminoso purifica
Tu cielo claro en claridad crecido.

Las aves hacia ti me han conducido,
Cuando el silencio el cántico amplifica,
Que en ti las luces íntimas explica,
Y esta pasión, primaveral latido.

El alma te construye entre azucenas
Sobre el paisaje que la brisa hiere,
Donde los aires tiemblan en tu ensueño.

Tu nombre vivo fluye por mis venas,
Y toda mi nostalgia te prefiere
En la espiga y la hierba de mi sueño.[9]

[9]After having included three sonnets of three different "Neo-classical" poets, so that the reader can have a yet more ample vision of the similarity of the poetry written by those of 1936, I will arbitrarily introduce here a typical sonnet of Dionisio Ridruejo, a poet decisively influenced by Bleiberg: "¡Qué cereal estío vigilante / se ciñe a ti, mientras la tierra abierta, / con la raíz de nuestra sombra muerta, / nos llama a sus entrañas anhelante! / Sube al cenit dorado del instante / esta sazón apenas descubierta / de tu carne y mi verbo, que despierta / en amorosos cauces incesante. / ¡Oh primavera de mi día breve! / Busca tú la palabra del sonido / que duda en labios de mi pulso leve. / Al aire en pie de luz, árbol y nido, / quiero fundar mi voz, la voz que debe / a tus íntimos ríos su sentido."

("What cereal vigilant summer / wraps around you, while the opened ground, / with the root of our dead shadow, / calls us desirously to its bowels! / This barely discovered season / of your flesh and my word, which awakens / incessantly in amorous river beds / rises to the golden zenith of the moment. / Oh Spring of my brief day! / You look for the word of the sound / which doubts on the lips of my light pulse. / In the air with the permanence of light, tree, and nest, / I want to found my voice, the voice which owes / its meaning to your intimate rivers.")

(While wounded by light and by hope,
my heart is thinking you and building you,
a luminous weeping purifies
your clear sky grown in clarity.

The birds have guided me toward you,
when silence amplifies the canticle
which explains the intimate lights in you,
and this passion, a Spring-like heartbeat.

My soul constructs you among lilies
on a landscape that the breeze wounds,
where the air trembles in your sleep.

Your living name flows through my veins,
and all my nostalgia prefers you
in the grain and grass of my dream.)

The separation from the loved one is painful, but paradoxically it is the creative force. Since poetry is dreaming about reality, it can only be written in a state of loneliness : "Y toda mi nostalgia te prefiere/En la espiga y la hierba de mi sueño" ("and all my nostalgia prefers you/in the grain and grass of my dream"). The landscape and each of its phenomena remind him of her, and *amada* and elements of Nature become fused : "El alma te construye entre azucenas/Sobre el paisaje que la brisa hiere" ("My soul constructs you among lilies/on a landscape that the breeze wounds"). Bleiberg's poetry also overflows with key words : almost always human characteristics associated with natural phenomena – *voz-viento* (voice-wind), *luz-miradas* (light-glances), *flor-dulzura* (flower-gentleness); and although he couches them in the mystery of fresh language, the reader soon grasps the poetic meaning of each. *Las miradas* of his love are engraved deeply in his memory and imagination, and all of his passion is concentrated in their contemplation. The image *ojos-miradas* (eyes-glances) is central in 15 of the 17 sonnets.

This sonnet is put together, both stylistically and structurally, in such a way that we never lose the relationship between "tú" and "yo" communicated by the poet. In his contemplative mood : "mi corazón te piensa y te edifica" ("my heart is thinking you and building you"); "El alma te construye entre azucenas" ("My soul constructs you among lilies"); and "Y toda mi nostalgia te prefiere" ("and all my nostalgia prefers you"). In his passionate mood : "Y esta pasión, primaveral latido" ("and this passion, a Spring-like heartbeat"); "Donde los aires tiemblan en tu ensueño" ("where the air trembles in your sleep"); and "Tu nombre vivo fluye por mis venas" ("Your living name flows through my veins"). The closing line of the first quartet : "Tu cielo claro en claridad crecido" is of a high order of prosody – the repetition of two words of the same root as part of a sustained alliteration, rhythmically ordered in a balanced iambic hendeca-syllable. In this connection we may add that the hendecasyllable is a flexible line which lends itself to various rhythms and tones. In this sonnet, Bleiberg delays the first heavy stress until the fourth syllable in lines 1, 2, 6, 8, 10, and 11. This variation of the sapphic hendecasyllable, which is predominant in all of the *Sonetos amorosos,* contributes to the tone of melancholy and gravity of his poetry. We will comment on the effect of another rhythm in the study of Hernández's poetry.

But beneath this world of order and form there is a feeling of uneasiness expressed by the poet which is something more than melancholy, and in order to best explain it, I will call your attention again to the use of antithesis : "el silencio amplifica el cántico" ("silence amplifies the canticle"); "el corazón herido por esperanza" ("the heart wounded by hope"); "la brisa hiere" ("the breeze wounds"). These examples are more suggestive than direct, but Bleiberg's poetry abounds with literal antitheses of words and almost every poem he writes is ambiguous in suggestion. Bleiberg transforms the classical antithetical theory of harmony into the vital and valiant recognition that each experience has its destructive as well as constructive effect. In turn, this realization is the source of anguish which he transfers to his poetic expression. From under the neo-classical form used by Bleiberg and from the middle of this Garcilasan-induced Arcadia, which on the second look is not really that at all, surges forth the voice of a romantic.

Now, latent in the *Sonetos amorosos* we are witness to a poetic credo that will underlie the book of poetry *Más allá de las ruinas* (1947) : the amorous experience is necessary to the writing of poetry, and it is sought not for its momentary joy, but more importantly so because it provides the only opportunity to affirm his existence. Poetry becomes the absolute expression of the temporal act of love and the poet feels the spiritual necessity to write and suffers from the anguish involved in expressing the ineffability of human emotions. The experience of four years in prison (the second part of *Más allá de las ruinas*) and the physical and mental hardships of his life immediately following his freedom intensify Bleiberg's existential anguish. In his post-war poetry he abandons his formalism, his *garcilasismo,* and his poetic expression overflows in long poems in free verse, characterized by the some-time use of colloquial language mixed with surrealistic imagery; or it is compressed in short, highly lyrical and musical songs, similar to those written by Miguel Hernández in prison. The themes are injustice, death, love, and solitude. If less violent in tone but deeper in psychological insight, the prison poems (1939–1943) of Bleiberg clearly belong to the type of poetry written by Dámaso Alonso in *Hijos de la ira.* In fact, it is worth drawing attention to a tradition that could be traced through the line *Sobre los ángeles-Más allá de las ruinas-Hijos de la ira.*

The radical solitude, or lack of presence, the feeling of unjust, but irremediable, abandonment led Bleiberg to meditate on existence and to decide that the mystery is solved only in the memory (in poetry) of the experience of life, poetically symbolized by the amorous experience. Bleiberg is more philosophical than his co-generationalists and the problem that confronts him constantly in this meditative and allusive, but violently anguished, poetry is the necessity to rescue the emotions that spring from the transitory experiences of life. For this reason his poetry is a product of experience, not of sentiment. The amorous experience is the encarnation of the ups and downs of human existence; and it helps him to passionately reject the distinction between life and death and between happiness and grief. Similar to Rilke in the *Duino Elegies,* death is for him the origin, and at the same time the very structure, of existence. That which is momentary in human experience is an expression of both life *and* death. But if death is the defining element of life, it follows that pain or grief must also be the fountain of happiness. Thus for Bleiberg, as for Rilke, poetry is lamentation, elegy.

Miguel Hernández (1910–1942) is certainly the most glorified poet of the group and the only one who has been studied with seriousness.[10] In a general study such as this there is very little original interpretation that might be added. The justification for including him in this essay lies mainly in the fact that critics hesitate as to whether they should consider him as indeed a member of the group of 1936 – because of his age and the date of his appearance on the literary scene of Madrid – or as an epigone of the Generation of 1927. If we have to classify him, I would tend toward the latter opinion, in spite of his formalism, or even because of its nature. However, even if the materials of his poetic reality are different, there are times when his preoccupation with existence coincides, in a very essential way, with that of Bleiberg, as the reader will clearly see. At any rate, a brief commentary on his work will, I believe, aid in a more total understanding of what the younger poets were doing in the 1930s.

Hernández is probably the only important twentieth-century Spanish poet formed outside the university, a significant fact in itself, although his self-learned knowledge of classical and Golden Age poetry was to shape his style. Of humble origins, he was a shepherd who abandoned his studies at the age of 14 and devoted his time to poetry. Attracted to Madrid in 1931, he went unnoticed in poetic circles and rejected, but not disheartened, he returned to Orihuela. A few years later he came back to Madrid and the publication of his *auto sacramental, Quien te ha visto y quien te ve,* and his book of poetry, *El rayo que no cesa* (1936), provided him with the recognition he had sought. His only love affair, that with his dressmaker wife, Josefina Manresa, was thwarted by continual absence and served as the inspiration for all of his good poetry. Biography and poetry are intimately related in Hernández. His humble and romantic life, his open defense of the leftist cause during the Civil War, his presentiment of death and his death in prison at age 32, all had a direct bearing on his poetry.

The early poems of Hernández, exemplified by the volume *Perito en lunas,* are written under the influence of Góngora and are little more than a revelation of a poet gifted with a facility of expression. In his struggle to find a more personal expression based on the poem and not poetics, Hernández progressively strips his poetry of conceptual conceits, and the final result is a book of exceptional lyrical quality, *Cancionero y Romancero de ausencias,* written in the same prison where Bleiberg was writing the *canciones* of *Más allá de las ruinas* and published posthumously.

[10]Studies on his poetry are included in the books of Concha Zardoya, Luis Cernuda and Vivanco on contemporary poetry. The most complete and profound study, however, is the excellent book of Juan Cano Ballesta, *La poesía de Miguel Hernández.* The complete works of Hernández, which contain every known poem he wrote, his theatre – including the propaganda plays he wrote for the Republican side – and some prose, have been published by Losada (1960).

Hernández does not idealize Nature or interiorize it like Bleiberg or Panero; he is a man of the earth, he is the *tierra*:

> Me llamo barro, aunque Miguel me llame
> > *(El rayo que no cesa, 15)*
> (My name is clay, even though I may be called Miguel)

> Aunque bajo la tierra
> mi amante cuerpo esté,
> escríbeme a la tierra
> que yo te escribiré.
> > ("A mi gran Josefina adorada")

> (Even though my loving body
> is under the earth,
> write me in care of the earth
> for I will write to you.)

He is constantly singing of the courage, dedication and virility of the real life of a shepherd, of a ploughman or of a torero, and his poetry is easily identified with the virtues of his race. It is this attachment to the popular aspects of Spanish life which forms the basis of the revolutionary tone attributed to the poetry of Hernández. Even during his attempt, almost pathetic according to some accounts, to incorporate himself into the cosmopolitan and cultural life of Madrid, and during his years in prison, he never succeeds in divorcing his expression from the attraction that the rural environment of his youth had for him. His imagery and his language are forever rooted in his concrete *vivencia* and the freshness and sincerity that run deep in his poetry give it one of its most lasting qualities. But although Hernández poeticized his loneliness in society and his desire to return to the simple life of Orihuela, he was also tormented by the eternal questions that elevate art above mere plain sincerity:

> Con tres heridas yo:
> la de la vida,
> la del amor,
> la de la muerte.
> > *(Cancionero y Romancero, 9)*

> (With three wounds am I:
> the one of life,
> the one of love,
> the one of death.)

El rayo que no cesa (1936), which consists of 29 Petrarchan sonnets with quevedesque touches and a long elegy in tercets written on the death of his friend Ramón Sijé, is the work of a poet who after the trials and tribulations of artisanry has forged an art which is distinctly his own. The fact that it was the third and definitive version – José María Cossío, friend and benefactor of Hernández, has published in Austral an edition with all the variants – reflects the discipline that the poet imposed on his decidedly facile expression. In these poems Hernández unleashes with inspiration and technical mastery an amorous sentiment which is both passionate and melancholic. A dionysiac conception of life and sensual love is punctured by absence and presages of physical death. In this exists the tragic note of Hernández's poetry. His reaction to the injustices of his separation from all that is sensual is very seldom resignation, but rather anger : he is impetuous and rebellious like the bull that symbolically appears so often in his verses. Nevertheless, from time to time, he lapses into a meditative mood and the constant play between valor and defeat, between sensuality and emptiness, lends a vital tension to his lyricism :

> Como el toro he nacido para el luto
> y el dolor, como el toro estoy marcado
> por un hierro infernal en el costado
> y por varón en la ingle con un fruto.
>
> Como el toro lo encuentro diminuto
> todo mi corazón desmesurado,
> y del rostro del beso enamorado,
> como el toro a tu amor se lo disputo.
>
> Como el toro me crezco en el castigo,
> la lengua en corazón tengo bañada
> y llevo al cuello un vendaval sonoro,
>
> Como el toro te sigo y te persigo,
> y dejas mi deseo en una espada,
> como el toro burlado, como el toro.

(Like the bull I was born for mourning
and suffering, like the bull I was marked
on the side by an infernal branding-iron
and because I am a man in the groin with a fruit.

Like the bull I find small
all my huge heart,
and enamoured by the face of the kiss
like the bull I contend with your love for it.

Like the bull I grow with punishment,
my tongue is bathed in my heart
and around my neck I wear a sonorous southwester,

Like the bull I follow you and I pursue you,
and you leave my desire on a sword,
like the deceived bull, like the bull.)

The anaphora or the repetition of a word or phrase throughout is very characteristic of Hernández; and in some cases, even more so than in the poem under discussion, it provides the principal unifying force; thus giving a musical lilt to the otherwise rigid sonnet form. As an example I will quote the first quartet of another sonnet from *El rayo que no cesa* :

> Fuera menos penado si no fuera
> nardo tu tez para mi vista, nardo,
> cardo tu piel para mi tacto, cardo,
> tuera tu voz para mi oído, tuera.

We sense that the sonnets of Hernández have a different rhythm than those of the other poets of his generation and if we resort to the simple metrical study of the hendecasyllable that aided us in a description of Bleiberg's poetry, we find that in lines 1, 2, 3, 5, 7, 8, 9, 12 and 14 the first stress is on the third syllable. This is the so-called melodic hendecasyllable, the most musical because of its balanced inflexion, and it is prevalent in all of the sonnets of Hernández. The metaphor of the *toro* which grows angrier and stronger in the face of death is central in *El rayo que no cesa* to describe the virility and the courageous sentiments of the poet. "El rayo que no cesa" ("The thunderbolt which never relents"), which is the pain of love caused by absence, is almost always given a metallic quality *cuchillo* (knife), *espada* (sword), *hierro* (iron) that materializes the pain and allows Hernández to pursue the imagery of the fate of the bull. In contrast to Rosales and Bleiberg, he does have the tendency – probably due to his apprenticeship in *gongorismo* – to sustain his imagery. The excellent structure of this sonnet can be best defined by the parallelism in *dolor-hierro-castigo* (suffering-branding iron-punishment) and in *marcado-desmesurado-burlado* (marked-huge-deceived) which are correlated respectively to *espada* (sword) and *corazón* (heart), and both sets of which are in turn correlated to *como el toro* (like the bull). This order, typically Petrarchan, has been studied by Carlos Bousoño elsewhere in the poetry of Hernández and is also patent in the work of Bleiberg, Rosales and Panero. For the primitive mind of Hernández – and I do not say this in the pejorative sense, because, as with García Lorca, the personalism and the originality of his poetry derives from this – there is no room for idealized sentiments : reality must be tangible. If he is preoccupied by philosophical problems of existence, they can only be expressed through what he feels sensually.

After his apprenticeship in Góngora and Calderón, *El rayo que no cesa* represents the beginning of the poetry of Hernández which was to give him a place among the best of contemporary Spain. He rapidly fell under the influence of Pablo Neruda and Aleixandre and found that his emotions, of a cosmic order, were best expressed in long poems of irregular versifications. In one way, the popular element of Hernández's poetry belongs to that of García Lorca and Alberti, but in his "popular" poetry the *I,* the individual struggle with existence (in reality, only poeticized as something collective), is much more present than in the poetry of the 1920's.

In conclusion, then, we can detect a general framework which might be used to characterize the poetry of the group of 1936. With them the return to "humanized" poetry in Spain becomes solidified. They are all love poets, but the paradoxical and antithetical conditions of the amorous experience only force a confrontation with the meaning of existence. The omnipresence of death, which they see as the ultimate meaning of life, runs throughout their poetry. It is the temporal condition of man, the fear of being lost and forgotten – "náufragos", all of them, as they reiterate time and time again – that most characterizes their lyric expression. Be this as it may, each individual poet discussed, as we have seen, escapes the bounds of his "poetic" generation to create an original expression of an intensely lyrical attitude.

Vassar College

Miguel Hernández:
Poet of Clay and of Light*

MANUEL DURAN

"Potato face", Pablo Neruda would affectionately call him. And Hernández – accurately, implacably – insists on defining himself as made of earth: "Me llamo barro aunque Miguel me llamo. / Barro es mi profesión y mi destino / que mancha con su lengua cuanto lame." "My name is clay even though Miguel is my name. Clay is my profession and my destiny that stains with its tongue all that it licks." Clay, yes, but rain, wind, hurricane, cataclysm, a lightning flash too. A blinding flash of lightning. Incessant, astonishing, dazzling flash of lightning. "The boy wonder from Orihuela" Juan Ramón Jiménez dubbed him in recognition of the 1934 publication of his religious play, *Quien te ha visto y quien te ve y sombra de lo que eras*. And more recently, in 1965, in *Literatura española contemporánea*, Ricardo Gullón, referring to those years in which the poet suddenly dominated the Madrid cliques, states precisely:

> The literary magazines afforded undeniable proofs of his talent and his infrequent poems (infrequent at that time) contributed to the formation of his legend. In them may be heard a voice of great refinement, a whole and genuine man whose expressive capacity allowed him to sound out vigorous and subtle songs of fine and musical modulations. A spontaneous Baroque style coincided with an emotion springing from the deep layers of that same *tierra-pueblo* from which the poet was formed. In an epoch like the present, when the popular is frequently a passing fad, how surprising to find it embodied in such high nobility and authenticity.[1]

Clay and light, yes. But in order to adhere to the essence of the poet, shaped by lively contrasts, one must carry the note to its extreme : the most clay-like clay yet unearthed; the most subtle and complex light ever envisioned. In his life the primordial clay is not earth alone, but also something more vital, and more

*Originally published in *Symposium* XXII (1968), and now revised by the author. Translation is by Katherine Meech.

[1]*Literatura española contemporánea* (eds. Ricardo Gullón and George D. Schade; New York, C. Scribner's Sons, 1965), p. 584.

difficult to poetize; it is dung. And the light dissolves in our hands – or before our eyes, impalpable – in a mist of gongorine, iridescent, transparent cobwebs through whose center a luminous robust axis rotates unceasingly. That is to say : the clay from which the poet is formed is something more than clay – more abrasive, rougher – than can possibly be imagined; and, yet more impossible and miraculous, is the complex permeating light toward which it aspires and reaches. Apropos of *Perito en lunas*, Concha Zardoya – one of the finest critical minds of Spanish literature, and, who, moreover, knows Hernández in depth – has written that the poet :

> tries to eliminate the original coarseness he believes himself to have, and fully achieves it. He is the man of the soil who aspires to the most cultured forms of expression, including the most refined. As Miguel writes this book he is overcoming a tragedy : that of the poet lacking culture who aspires to the most elevated forms of thought and art. No critic has observed in this book what there is in it of human drama. If they had only seen the house in which Miguel lived, they would have understood this first reaction against the dung surrounding him. (*Poesía española contemporánea*, p. 647.)

It's not enough to know – intellectually, superficially – that Miguel Hernández was a shepherd. A thousand absurdly literary, false, useless images intervene between our understanding and the reality. To be a shepherd – and a poor shepherd – means to lead a miserable and dirty life. To smell of cattle. To clean stables. But let the poet explain for himself, in a prose piece which remained unedited until Concha Zardoya published it in her book : he wrote it in those years when he was preparing *Perito en lunas,* and it is entitled "Miguel y mártir".

> Every day with all my dignity I fling the dung from the cattle stalls which I sweep clean with the palm-leaf broom. Every day the udders rise to my dignity until I stoop to produce foam, transient milk bubbles; the water in the well goes ever lower; the critical situation of my life's function, more ugly for being offensive and odorous; the obstacles of dung which I encounter strewn along the road from my house to my orchard; the things I touch; the beings to whom I grant my world of images; the temptation into which I fall, antonio (sic).
> Every day I'm becoming sanctified, martyred and mute.

And Concha Zardoya comments :

> From this moment, Miguel's entire life will be an unceasing effort to elevate all the sad and ugly things besieging his existence by dint of his inner dignity and his sense of beauty. Now more than herder of the family goats, he will be "lunicultor", "expert in moons".

To dignify does not mean – never did mean for Miguel Hernández, always faithful to his origins, to his childhood and adolescence – to erase and forget. On the contrary. His fidelity to the soil, to the clay – to the impure, stained clay –

will remain a constant in his poetry. One of the best poems from *Viento del pueblo* – a poem with autobiographical savor – is his ode to "Niño yuntero", in which he sings of the humble infant born amidst manure, and on singing of him he praises all poor children who have known hunger and misery : "Entre estiércol puro y vivo / de vacas trae a la vida / un alma color de olivo / vieja ya y encallecida". "Amid the pure and living manure of cows he is brought into life with an olive-colored soul that is already old and calloused." And in the opening poem to García Lorca, he tells us that the assassinated poet will forever be "estiércol padre de la madreselva", "dung father to the honey-suckle". And in Hernández' plays we encounter equal fidelity to the realism of the soil, cattle, daily life : the suspicious laborer, Quintín, sings in *El labrador de más aire* :

> En los templados establos
> donde el amor huele a paja,
> a honrado estiércol y a leche,
> hay un estruendo de vacas
> que se enamoran a solas
> y a solas rumian y braman.
> Los toros de las dehesas
> las oyen dentro del agua
> y hunden con ira en la arena
> sus enamoradas astas.

> (In the tempered stables
> where love has the odor of straw,
> honest manure, and milk,
> there is an uproar among the cows
> that fall in love by themselves,
> and by themselves ruminate and bellow.
> The bulls of the pastures
> hear them inside the water
> and angrily plunge
> their enamored horns into the sand.)

Faithfulness to his origins, always. Even when he begins to forge ahead. Toward the middle of 1935 Vicente Aleixandre's *La destrucción o el amor* is published. Miguel knows it to be an important book; perhaps he already knows one of the poems; perhaps he has seen the book in a friend's house. But – as always – he hasn't money even for the most indispensable things. He writes a letter to the author requesting the book. The letter is the beginning of a deep friendship; Aleixandre is one of his masters, and Miguel will dedicate to him his "Oda entre arena y piedra a Vicente Aleixandre". Miguel's letter is signed : "Miguel Hernández, goatherd of Orihuela". (Wasn't there a certain coquetry, conscious or unconscious, in this phrase? The shepherd – a poet who was increasingly more a poet and less a shepherd. And nevertheless, his practical knowledge of peasant life is a constant in his poetry, and one of the deepest and most significant ingredients.)

And constancy to suffering. Miguel had suffered in Orihuela. An indication of it for us is the testimony of the poet himself and that of his friends. It is sufficient, for example, to re-read a paragraph from the letter García Lorca writes to him shortly after publication of *Perito en lunas*; a letter found by Concha Zardoya in the private archives of Josefina Manresa, the poet's widow, and published in the July-September issue of the *Bulletin Hispanique* in 1958.

> My dear poet : I haven't forgotten you. But I live to the fullest and my letter-writing pen slips from my hands. I remember you vividly because I know that you are suffering from those porcine people who surround you and I grieve to see your vital and luminous strength penned up in the corral and being buffeted along the walls. . . .

The effort toward his poetic "conversion" drained him, isolating him from his normal climate without opening doors to other milieus for him; the poet complained of the silence greeting his book, and Federico tries to calm him.

> People are unjust. *Perito en lunas* doesn't deserve that stupid silence, no. It deserves attention and stimulation and the love of good people. You have that and you will have that because yours is poet's blood, even when you protest in your letter, in the midst of brutal things (which I like), you have the tenderness of your luminous and tormented heart.

Miguel was to continue suffering – and loving – in Madrid, without ever completely acclimatizing himself to life in the great city. He was to suffer and tremble with indignation during the Civil War. The beginning of the war must have had for Hernández an especially bitter savor : Juan Cano Ballesta in his excellent book on *La poesía de Miguel Hernández* tells us that :

> In Elda on August 13, 1936 the civil guard Manuel Manresa, the father of Josefina (the poet's betrothed), dies after being shot in the head. He is assassinated in the heart of the city by the Republican militiamen on whose side Miguel Hernández was fighting.[2]

A hard trial, a personal drama fusing into the collective drama. The poet's "bloody fate" is now outlined. There are many poems written between 1935 and 1939 in which a premonition of disaster, of imminent death, of urgency, of anguish is transparent. The poet wants to find himself, and find others, before dying. He has a presentiment that his life will end badly and the passion that bursts out in *Viento del pueblo* – containing some of his best poems – will break, to transform itself into ashes and tears. Not in vain is the poet also, and before all else, a *vates*, a soothsayer. Miguel foresees his own tragic death and the tragic death of the Republic which has given wings to his voice. And thus is born this confused and suffering, uneven and at times grandiose, book that is *El hombre acecha*. Cano Ballesta writes :

[2]Juan Cano Ballesta, *La poesía de Miguel Hernández* (Madrid, 1962), p. 45.

The poet slowly penetrates his own being, the purifying fire of grief stripping him of everything that might be mere superficial wordiness with neither message nor depth. In *El hombre acecha* one catches a glimpse of the fatal and tragic unravelling of the War. Bitterness, the hatred of man for man, bares its claws in these poems . . . the hands which in *Viento del pueblo* were still tools, messages of the soul, sources of life and richness, have become instruments of destruction, *claws* of hate. The valiant soldier, carefree youth, the day laborer, have remembered their claws, have metamorphosed into tigers : man lurks in wait for man. The same war which in *Viento del pueblo* was enthusiasm, courage, heroism, paean to happiness, has changed into endless tragedy : hatreds, wounds, hospitals, hunger and jails.[3]

It is precisely this individual and collective anguish, an anguish that would eventually consume him, which lends his poetry of these years a dimension that no other contemporary Spanish poet has. We feel that the poems of his books written during the War – and among them we of course include the beautiful *Cancionero y romancero de ausencias,* a book written amidst the war, amidst the painful consequences of a war that the conquerors meant to prolong for years and years in the hearts of all Spaniards – yield a strange, a unique conjunction of past, present and future. Past, because the classical Spanish culture is present – Quevedo, Góngora, Lope, Calderón – in many of Miguel's lines. Present, because Miguel's war poetry is unique : if at some moment the poet has fully been a witness, this obtains in his case. A witness who participates in and lives each instant, who transforms each tragic moment into perennial poetry. And future, because in his enthusiastic or bitter visions, Miguel was ahead of his contemporaries, and foresaw or feared what was about to happen; moreover, his attitude and the themes chosen by him prefigured the evolution of Spanish lyric poetry in the following decades.

One must not forget the fundamental fact that Hernández belonged – along with Leopoldo Panero, Luis Rosales, Luis Felipe Vivanco, Germán Bleiberg, Ildefonso-Manuel Gil – to the so-called "generation of the Republic" – or, as many prefer, to the so-called "Generation of '36". Let us defer, for a more opportune occasion, the decision as to whether one may designate the group of writers who begin to publish in those years a "generation". (On the "Generation of '36", see the July-August issue of *Insula,* 1965.) All these poets have something in common : in those years the cult of Garcilaso replaces the cult of Góngora, dominant throughout the "generation of the Dictatorship" or that of '27, or that of '28 – as it would be more logical to count if we situate a generation at thirty years' distance from the preceding, the year '28 being the exact date following 1898. And almost all of them are conventionally religious poets. Almost all, *but not Miguel,* anchored in the imminent, in the "here and now", and, moreover, shaken by the "viento del pueblo", by the passion of blood, the creation and the destruction of everything human and by social and

[3] Juan Cano Ballesta, p. 48.

73

political passion.[4] There is no attempt made here to denigrate the other poets of Hernández' generation. Great poems have issued from the pen of Panero or Rosales. But if we ask ourselves sincerely – whatever our political position or our religious belief may be – what is the most characteristic attitude of our epoch – not only of these last few years, but including our entire century – politics or religiosity, I believe the answer to be rather obvious. The political fervor, the impassioned interest in themes stirred up by politics not only has exploded on more than one occasion, but has permeated all countries, old or new, throughout the century. And if in these last few years, there has been – as Raymond Aron and others have noted – a certain chilling of ideological passions, this is true particularly with respect to European countries and is not applicable to the majority of remaining countries. At any rate, the evolution of Spanish poetry was going to prove Hernández right. Let us think of Crémer, Celaya, Blas de Otero, Angela Figuera. Let us recall how Celaya curses "la poesía concebida como un lujo/cultural por los neutrales", "the poetry conceived by neutrals as a cultural luxury", and how Crémer rebukes the "pure" poets : "It is a crime to warble rhythmically while other men, without fanfare, work, suffer and die." Of all the poets of his generation, the only one who from the very first moment, from the very first reading of any one of his books, it would be inconceivable to place outside our century is Hernández. In him there is a deep tragic perception of life, not motivated by metaphysics, but rooted in existential experiences and premonitions : for Hernández, life is always threatened :

> Un carnívoro cuchillo
> de ala dulce y homicida
> sostiene un vuelo y un brillo
> alrededor de mi vida.

Or, as Edwin Honig translates :

> Some flesh-eating knife
> on tender killing wings
> hovers steadily, flashing
> down upon my life.

And this sensation of life as menaced, precarious, difficult, painful, is perhaps the sensation most typical of our time and which best helps to define our century.

Because one must specify : our century, the Twentieth Century, we know, is not – cannot be – identical with the Nineteenth Century. Romanticism – and

[4]Of course we are referring to his mature poetry. His background and his friends, especially Ramón Sijé, are genuinely Catholic, and this is reflected in some of his early poems and in his religious play *Quien te ha visto y quien te ve y sombra de lo que eras.* Concha Zardoya observes the way in which communion, which in Calderón's religious plays is so theatrical and deified, becomes in Hernández' play "human, intimate, and almost domesticated while a delightful rustic aroma envelops it" (*El mundo poético de Miguel Hernández*, Madrid, 1960, p. 89). And Juan Cano Ballesta: "The poet reveals in his play that he is acquainted with matters of Christian faith such as the mystery of the Eucharist, grace, redemption, forgiveness. What he had never learned in school he was undoubtedly able to acquire from the deep truths of Calderonian religious plays" (p. 31).

the last manifestation, the last avatar, the definitive version of Romanticism is "Modernism" – dominates all of the last century. But the last century ends not in 1899 nor in 1900, as calendars or our "geometric spirit" would lead us to believe, but rather, naturally, in 1914. By 1918 – or 1919 in some countries – we change emotional and cultural climates. What previously was delicate, sweet – and today it seems to us excessively, cloyingly sweet – has become bitter, intense, acid. Satire, caricature, and irony seize control of the forefront, displacing previously dominant elements. The evolution can be seen in clear and precise form, in Spanish literature, if we examine the profound changes that made Valle-Inclán's evolution possible; between the *Sonatas,* written according to the best Modernist precepts, and the *esperpentos,* reflecting irony, love of the grotesque, and social and political criticism so fitting and characteristic of our century, there is stylistically, aesthetically, an abyss. And nevertheless the agile Valle-Inclán makes the mortal leap over the abyss in a few years, precisely – and not by chance – in the years 1916 to 1919. Let us think of *La lámpara maravillosa, La pipa de kif,* and *Los cuernos de Don Friolera* : the succession – the evolution – is demonstrative, dazzling, illuminating. If we do not appreciate that Valle's evolution, in those brief years, exemplifies – symbolizes, encapsulates – the evolution of romantic styles toward the typically modern – existential, ironic, bold, tragic – we shall not be able to understand thoroughly any of the remaining phenomena typifying the literature of our time. And it's not possible either to forget that the other great definers of the end of an epoch and the beginning of ours – Proust, Kafka, Mann – are getting ready to give us their sentimental photograph of the past or their blueprint of the future as envisioned precisely around these years.

The grand theme, then, developed by the most typical authors of our century *is the theme of precarious, menaced, unstable life.* Proust speaks to us, at the end of his great novel, of a meeting of phantoms. In regard to Kafka, his cruel, acid tone, manifests itself most clearly. And irony is the preferred weapon of Joyce and Mann. All of them tell us the same story : the degradation of myths – grandiose or sentimental – which Romanticism had exalted – and that almost always reached us from much farther afield. Miguel Hernández has not broken completely with the Romantic tradition. (This is also true, if one tries to be precise, with respect to Surrealism, inheritor of the great current coming from German Romanticism, passing through Baudelaire and Rimbaud, visionary poets, and flowing into Apollinaire, Aragon, Eluard, Breton and so many others, among whom were Vallejo and Neruda; and it is well known how deep the influence of Neruda was on Hernández.) The tone of Miguel's poetry is existentialist – tragic. It toys neither with situations nor words (which was typical of a certain stage of the Vanguard, and of some writers of its initial period, during the Twenties : let us think of the early Gerardo Diego, or of Gómez de la Serna's *greguerías*). On the contrary : he has discovered that life is a serious game, totally and profoundly serious :

> Escribí en el arenal
> los tres nombres de la vida :
> vida, muerte, amor.

75

I wrote on the sand
the three names of life :
Life, death, love.

If we think of the Hernández on the threshold of the Civil War, shortly before the great collective tragedy, and we re-read the poems he wrote in those months, we will sense that the poet already intuited what was going to happen, he lived it beforehand in his heart. As Cano Ballesta, one of the critics who has most accurately interpreted Hernández, points out :

> ... this possible Hernandian existentialism, far from having its inspiration in Heidegger or in any other philosophical school, is rather fully experienced, Hispanic existentialism, an existentialism *avant la lettre,* a product perhaps of a certain fatalism and of that peculiarly Hispanic assimilation of time flowing into the immediate from the present. As Christoph Eich aptly notes (in *Federico García Lorca, poeta de la intensidad,* pp. 123-124), Spaniards were existentialists before Kierkegaard and before Existentialism was a philosophy and a fashion. The obsessive idea of the constant threat of the flesh-eating knife circling about his life could have come to Miguel Hernández perhaps from Fate's continual blows affecting his hapless existence – let us recall the dismal event inspiring *Sino sangriento* – or perhaps from the fatalist Andalusian vision moulded on the knives and razors of gypsy life and García Lorca's dramas that Miguel knew well. (op. cit., p. 65).

Unstable life begins, for European society, in 1914. And this is the date when the great aesthetic currents of the Nineteenth Century end. Everything happening after 1914 is "contemporary". And one of the fundamental characteristics of the contemporary is instability, the realization that everything – society, economy, philosophic ideas – is precarious. This sensation does not establish itself suddenly; it insinuates itself little by little; the first reaction of writers and artists is one of a happy and hopeful nihilism; only in the "Thirties" with the second wave of anguish and instability, unleashed worldwide by the economic depression of 1929, do we begin to see in outline a frankly pessimistic and anguished attitude. (Those who feel sceptical in regard to those ideas may read the lucid pages written by Lucien Goldmann concerning the esthetic evolution of André Malraux, one of the most representative authors of the "Thirties" : in addition I dare to suggest that Malraux, Hernández and Stephen Spender are with all probability the most typical authors of the "Spirit of the Thirties".

It has been said that poetry is "what gets lost in translation." There is enough truth in this definition to give pause to anyone trying to communicate some aspects of Hernández' art to an English-speaking audience.

A possible solution might be to compare the Spanish poet to an American or English poet of the same generation and of roughly similar sensitivity. The task is far from easy. A poet is nothing if not an individualist. Comparing two poets belonging to different cultures is perhaps like trying to add apples and pears. Yet it has to be attempted. Not every American or English poet of the Thirties will do. Perhaps the one who comes closest to Hernández in his awareness of a violent and unhappy period is W. H. Auden.

Auden is almost by definition *the* poet of the Thirties – more specifically of the late Thirties – in England, just as T. S. Eliot had been for the Anglo-Saxon world the poet of the Twenties and Dylan Thomas was to become the poet of the Forties.

F. R. Leavis had declared in 1932 that T. S. Eliot and Ezra Pound had jointly brought about a significant reorientation of literature. By the late Thirties neither Eliot nor Pound were as relevant as they once had been. Pound was sinking fast into a cranky underworld of his own making. Eliot was floating in the lofty, if somewhat lonely, heaven of Anglo-Catholicism. Only Auden – and occasionally Louis MacNeice – had found the right voice for those troubled years. As A. Alvarez has noted (in "English Poetry Today", included in *On Contemporary Literature,* edited by Richard Kostelanetz), "the Thirties poets reacted against those of the Twenties by asserting that they had no time to be difficult or inward or experimental; the political situation was too urgent. W. H. Auden gave them the go-ahead because he combined the extraordinary technical skill in traditional forms with an extraordinary feel for the most contemporary of contemporary idiom".

Hernández is also, when he feels like it, a virtuoso of classical forms, a technician of verse. He is also obsessed with the present, with violence, with cruelty. Their voices – the Spanish poet's, strong, earthy; the Englishman's well-modulated upper-class accent – are sometimes strikingly similar. Both pay close attention to the present – for both, politics are important – for both hope and despair intermingle. Auden writes :

> For private reasons I must have the truth, remember
> These years have seen a boom in sorrow;
> The presses of idleness issued more despair
>   And it was honoured,
> Gross Hunger took on more hands every month,
> Erecting here and everywhere his vast
>   Unnecessary workshops;
> Europe grew anxious about her health,
> Combines tottered, credits froze,
> And business shivered in a banker's winter
>   While we were kissing.
>   (XVII, *Look, Stranger!*)

Auden can be intense, bitter, desolate : "Love gave the power, but took the will." (XX, *Look, Stranger!*) Yet what separates Auden from Hernández turns out to be as important as the sensitivity they share. Auden's bent towards satire, irony, caricature, his love of understatement, brings him often to write what can be described only as "light verse" even when he is dealing with tragic situations :

> The dogs are barking, the crops are growing
> But nobody knows how the wind is blowing :

77

> Gosh, to look at we're no great catch;
> History seems to have struck a bad patch.
>
> We haven't the time – it's been such a rush –
> Except to attend to our own little push :
> The teacher setting examinations,
> The journalist writing his falsifications,
>
> The poet reciting to Lady Diana
> While the footmen whisper 'Have a banana',
> The judge enforcing the obsolete law,
> The banker making the loan for the war,
>
> The expert designing the long-range gun
> To exterminate everyone under the sun,
> Would like to get out but could only mutter;
> 'What can I do? It's my bread and butter'.

Auden's irony is effective. Yet we feel somehow far removed from the zone of danger, reassured by Auden's clever mixture of everyday language and technical terms borrowed from Freud and the economists, from the politicians and the journalists. We are spectators. We may worry, anguish may seep into our consciousness, but we keep on looking. Auden is the voyeur of the great disaster that engulfs the world in the late Thirties.

"Que la vie est quotidienne!" Jules Laforgue's words are an apt introduction to contemporary poetry. But there are many ways to emphasize the present. Auden is the sophisticated poet of city life. Hernández brings us back, time and again, to the desolate plains of Spain, to the present of villages, to the humble life of animals :

> Like the bull I was born to sorrow
> and pain; like the bull I am marked
> by a hellish brand in the ribs
> and a masculine fruit in the groin.
> > (*The Unending Lightning*, XXIII,
> > tr. by Edwin Honig)

The death of a close friend sends the Spanish poet into a demented frenzy :

> I want to dig the earth up with my teeth.
> ....
> I'll hollow out this pit until I find you,
> kiss your noble head, ungag your mouth,
> and bring you back to life.
> > (*Elegy for Ramón Sijé,* tr. by E. Honig)

Both Auden and Hernández are great poets who know how to cope with the presence of death and cruelty. For Auden the experience entails a loss of innocence : "The unjust walk the earth", and also "And England to our meditations seemed/The perfect setting :/But now it has no innocence at all", and

> Starving through the leafless wood
> Trolls run scolding for their food;
> And the nightingale is dumb,
> And the angel will not come.

Hernández never quite loses his innocence and his hope. Only towards the end, in his pathetic poem to his son, "Nanas de la cebolla", when the poet is dying in jail, after receiving a letter from his wife in which she wrote she had only bread and onion to eat, despair seems to engulf him. Yet he longs to escape into the happy unconsciousness of childhood, hopes also his own son will avoid becoming conscious of the cruelty and oppression surrounding him. "Don't even know what happens or what goes on" : the pain had become unendurable, the poet needed a moment of respite. Yet the greatness of Hernández, and that of Auden, is based partly on the fact that each one of them tried to make his readers fully aware of what was going on.

Life continually lashes out at Hernández in cruel and rapid blows, there isn't time; no time to resist elastically, to assimilate the circumstances, to adapt and be able to smile again. There isn't time. This is, precisely, the anguished message. And time is precisely what superabounds *before* Hernández : it is in excess to the point where the poet can stop, morosely, and, reflecting – Machado, Juan Ramón – try to grasp the essence of time : try to discover what time means. But in the decade of the Thirties everything accelerates. If we recall the years of the Republic and the Civil War, we're shaken by their strange resemblance to one of those old films where everyone moves convulsively (and those who have seen the movie *Mourir à Madrid* will remember that politicians were not the only ones who lived and died by brusque blows of destiny).

Love, life, death, sexuality, liberty. These are Miguel's compass points. Sex is a weapon, it must act to penetrate into history, to fashion a cleaner future for the children we dream about; sensuality has a dimension that goes far beyond concrete and subjective – always egotistical – experience; Góngora would not perhaps have been able to foresee the future of sensuality; but in any case, Miguel Hernández does so for him; it is so handled that sensations may vibrate like a chord expanding indefinitely, limitlessly : the world is written in cipher, as Fray Luis de León knew and – after the esthetic revolution of the Romantics – the Symbolists and "Modernists", Ruben Darío and Juan Ramón Jiménez. The world is written in cipher, *but the key which opens the secret doors is not amusement, pleasure or play; it is suffering.* And suffering and poetry tend increasingly to merge for Miguel. As José Albi has seen :

> His poetic compass and his human compass approximate more and more to each other (in his last work, the *Cancionero*) and the two forces that propel his creative capacity – life and death – continually manifest themselves in all their vigor. On the one hand the pull of the land, essentially

79

no more than a call toward death, a return to origins. On the other hand it is life, felt through love and liberty, that illuminates the well of energy in his soul. Life and death attract and repel each other with equal force. But something that is life, and, at the same time, a little of death, conquers. It is love. ("El último Miguel" : *Verbo,* Dec. 1954, Alicante)

Urgency is one of the poet's themes. It is the one that organizes and orchestrates the poet's anguish. And, above it, *ambiguity* : the poet must see and feel clearly; but his message must be complex and ambiguous because such is the reality he reflects : the light fights with the shadows, and although there's always a ray of light to conquer the shadow, it's also true the world has suddenly become a prison; hands may be chained wings, lightning flashes in form of wings, and, also, claws. And precisely urgency and ambiguity are two very characteristic notes of our century, during which all rhythms have dramatically accelerated, and all our traditional sources of beliefs and values have become obscured. All who may see today's world in totally univocal form, with neither shadows nor doubts, will be assured of enormous success in the propaganda offices of some political party or will earn high salaries in Madison Avenue offices where commercial propaganda is prepared, but none of this has anything to do with poets. We have urgency because history presses and stimulates us on all sides; we feel confused because the verities of the great religious and rationalist systems have slipped through our fingers. And all of it is inferred from an attentive reading of the cultural, political, social and economic events of our century, and of Miguel's best poems. This and no other is the message of the early Dámaso Alonso of the post-war period, with his Madrid that is a cemetery of more than one million corpses. The existential anguish permeating some of the poems from *Hijos de la ira,* although of religious root, also has its source in Hernández, or at least, if not source, a clear antecedent. It all signifies one thing : the poetic position of Hernández bridges the great span between the Thirties and the post-war epoch in Spain. A key position, therefore, although few have recognized his essential importance.

The existential poetry of Dámaso Alonso and the social poetry of Blas de Otero, Gabriel Celaya, of so many others; impossible to imagine them in the abstract, removed from the difficult and painful circumstances of Spanish post-war life. But it is also impossible, or very difficult, to avoid recalling that in all these cases – in all these poetic trends – Miguel Hernández has been the precursor. The authentic poet of the years of the Republic, the most representative, he is also the only one who was capable of projecting his poetic vision toward the future, and having fully lived the war years and the tragedy of the post-war period, could express the desperation and the hope that are still the two great poles of Spanish poetry today.

Criticism has been less than generous with Miguel Hernández's work. The two basic works continue to be Concha Zardoya's study, published first by the Hispanic Institute in 1955 and partially reproduced later in *Poesía española contemporánea* (in the Guadarrama series), and Cano Ballesta's book (in Gredos). We also have Dario Puccini's excellent essays on Hernández. The bibliography in Cano Ballesta's book consists of 59 works on the poet's life and work. It is not much if we compare it with what has been published on other great poets of our century. The explanation for this is to be found in part in Spain's official attitude, for many years, hostile to what the poet represented. (Juan Cano Ballesta, a colleague of mine at Yale University, has told me how difficult it was to work on the subject : open hostility on the part of the authorities, impossibility of consulting certain texts without violating the regulations, etc.) And outside Spain critical attention seems to have been polarized by other great figures surrounding the poet in his time. To give a concrete example : the bibliography of PMLA for 1966 – not exhaustive, but painstaking, and certainly a good barometer of collective preference – gives us one *single article* for this year on Miguel Hernández.

All of this, naturally, matters little. We now have very detailed and valuable studies on the poet's life and work. We have his poetry. In spite of the incompleteness of his "complete works" they perpetuate themselves, endure, make themselves felt. No shadow will have the power to conquer them : they will last as long as the Spanish language lasts and as long as our awareness lasts of what it truly is to be a man, rooted in the clay and hurtling toward the unattainable like a flash of light.

Yale University

The Poetry of Leopoldo Panero[*]

JAIME FERRAN

In the symposium at Syracuse University on "La generación del '36", the figure of Miguel Hernández was highlighted to the point that three talks were devoted to it.[1] That was in part because critical interpretation is better equipped to deal with a vanished poet, with his work irremediably cut short or ended, than in the case of a poet alive and often changing. This paper today proposes to focus on another poet, Leopoldo Panero, who died only a few years ago. In this span, various instruments have been added to those which we already had to study this vanished poet and friend. In the first place, the number which *Insula* practically devoted to him in the year of his death.[2] In the second instance, an almost complete edition of his work.[3] Lastly, the special volume which the review *Cuadernos Hispanoamericanos*[4] dedicates to him and covers significant lacunae in his edited work through the publication by his son of some hitherto unedited poems.

Now it is becoming clear – and the book for which these pages are destined may perhaps contribute to the clarification – that in the "Generación del '36" two very distinct waves are present : one accelerated in development by the year giving title to the generation; the other, without ceasing to belong to the generation mentioned, delayed in its appearance by the historical circumstances of that year. Most clearly, Leopoldo Panero belongs to the former of these waves of a generation, to the group of poets formed by Bleiberg, Ridruejo, Rosales and Vivanco.

For both Hernández and Panero, the year evidently acted as a catalyst for their writing, and if they had previously slipped into the shadow of preoccupations impeding the creative writers of the preceding Generation of '27, they did strike out on a new road by '36. Suffice it to recall for what relates to Hernández, the leap from *Perito en lunas,* an eminently gongoristic book, to the works the poet wrote from 1936. The phenomenon can be observed in the

[*] Translated by Katherine Meech.

[1] Juan Cano Ballesta, "La renovación poética de los años treinta y Miguel Hernández"; Manuel Durán, "Miguel Hernández: poeta del barro y de la luz"; Javier Herrero, "Miguel Hernández: sangre y guerra"; see in *Symposium* XXII (Summer, 1968).
[2] *Insula,* No. 193 (December, 1962).
[3] Leopoldo Panero, *Poesía, 1932–1960,* Prol. Dámaso Alonso (Madrid, 1963).
[4] *Cuadernos Hispanoamericanos,* Nos. 187-188 (July-August, 1965).

case of Panero, in whom if we examine *Versos del Guadarrama* (1930 to 1939), we shall observe two epochs : the initial one, to which has been ascribed a radiant Guillenesque vitality, most clearly evident in poems such as the opening one, "Cumbre I" :

> Cumbre. La brisa tiembla
> desnuda como un lirio.
> Mañana estremecida
> pura y fresca en los pinos.[5]
>
> ....
>
> (Summit. The breeze trembles
> naked like a lily.
> A quivering morning
> pure and fresh in the pinetrees.)

If we compare this poem with what follows, "Cumbre II" (1930), we shall see that the Guillenesque ascription wears thin. In the last two strophes of the poem, a procedure of parenthetic asides, reinforced by exclamation marks, serves to introduce an eminently objective attitude – the contemplation of the summit – the subjective world of the poet : a Guillenesque device in origin, but treated by Panero in a distinctly personal manner :

> Los barrancos sin nadie.
> (¡Mi corazón en sueños
> era inmenso !) La noche :
> limpidez del silencio.
>
> Cumbre pura y fragante.
> Mi corazón soñaba
> desvelado en la sombra.
> (¡Y era inmensa mi alma !)[6]
>
> (Deserted ravines.
> (My heart in dreams
> was immense !) Night :
> Purity of the silence.
>
> The pure and fragrant summit.
> Wide-awake in the shadows
> my heart was dreaming.
> (And my soul was immense.))

The influence of Guillén on Panero has been mentioned by Gullón in *Insula*[7]

[5] Panero, p. 47.
[6] Panero, p. 48.
[7] *Insula*, No. 193, p. 10.

and in *Cuadernos Hispanoamericanos*[8], but it is appropriate that we link with it from the beginning this subjective presence that permeates the poem and doubtless has given ground for Rosales to speak later of the poet's "new humanism".[9] Here follow a few extracts from the *Versos del Guadarrama,* confirming the wedding of the external with the subjective, previously mentioned :

> se extiende mi dolor en la penumbra
> del campo...............................[10]

> (My pain spreads out in the deep shadows
> of the countryside. . . .)

> Y el corazón silencia levemente
> su palabra más pura, y su retama
> se alza en dorado vuelo............[11]

> (And there my heart gently silences
> the purest word, while yellow flowers
> rise in golden flight. . . .)

> ....Dios nos puso
> dentro del corazón la tierra entera[12]

> (God put
> inside our hearts the entire world.)

The external and the subjective, or as the poet himself would rather say, "in this hope, which is like a continuation of the reality of each day"[13], we shall hear the best Panero, a voice still pledged to the shadow of the initial Guillenesque passion, while approaching a more personal tone through the union of the two aspects.

This technique perhaps culminates in the two tercets of the sonnet "Tras la sombra de un día", where the final illuminative parenthesis reinforces the total meaning of the poem :

> Hoy escucho al pasar junto a tu hondura
> mi propio corazón, mi furia triste,
> y el aullar de los pinos en el viento. . . .

> ¡Oh roto Guadarrama tras la oscura
> penumbra del pinar que el cierzo embiste !
> (. . . mientras fluye ya eterno el pensamiento.)[14]

[8]*Cuadernos Hispanoamericanos,* Nos. 187-188, p. 161.
[9]*Ibid.,* p. 35.
[10]Panero, p. 49.
[11]Panero, p. 50.
[12]Panero, p. 52.
[13]*Cuadernos Hispanoamericanos,* Nos. 187-188, p. 14.
[14]Panero, p. 56.

(Today while passing alongside your depths
I listen to my own heart, my sad fury,
and the howling of the pinetrees in the wind. . . .

Oh broken Guadarrama beyond the dark
shadows of the pine forests lashed by the north wind.
(. . . while thought, already eternal, flows on.))

Continuing with the *Versos del Guadarrama*, Panero offers two significant sonnets : "Por donde van las águilas", dated 1936, and "Materia transparente", dated 1939. We see, first, that the poet has rejected the hendecasyllable, which had predominated in the sonnets and in the *silvas*. He now prefers the alexandrine as if in the longer verse measure he might grasp the significance blazing before his eyes. The first sonnet also introduces an anticipation of elements in conflict and the favorite Panerian solution :

> Tengo miedo. Levanto los ojos. Dios azota
> mi corazón. El vaho de la nieve se enfría
> lo mismo que un recuerdo.................[15]

(I am afraid. I lift my eyes. God flogs
my heart. The snow's vapors turn cold
the same as a memory . . .)

Secondly there is this extreme, familiar solution :

> Otra vez como en sueños mi corazón se empaña
> de haber vivido . . . ¡Oh fresca materia transparente !
> De nuevo como entonces siento a Dios en mi entraña,
> Pero en mi pecho ahora es sed lo que era fuente.[16]

(Once more as though in dreams my heart is filled with gloom
from having lived . . . Oh matter that is fresh and transparent.
Again, as in the past, I feel God deep inside,
But in my breast, what was once a fountain is now thirst.)

The whiplash of the Civil War once spent, the poetry of Panero now seeks the favored hendecasyllable and displays the second clearly recognizable influence in his work, that of Federico García Lorca's octosyllabic ballads, as in "Camino del Guadarrama" : and more especially in the one dedicated to "Joaquina Márquez" (1930-1939), which permits us to trace this second influence across those years when the poet happily concluded his first collected works.

There is, then, in the initial Panero the slight influence of two poets from the preceding generation, those of Jorge Guillén and Federico García Lorca.

[15] Panero, p. 57.
[16] Panero, p. 58.

Nevertheless these first two supports, in the ascent toward his own voice, have much less significance than the subsequent presence of Antonio Machado in the work of Panero. Here, with the inexorable law fulfilled of the rebellion against the father, in favor of the grandfather, Panero is seen selecting and incorporating the best of the Machadian experience.

Although there has been exaggeration in treating this presence in Panero, there undoubtedly exists a kinship of expression that in no way lessens Panerian originality. Perhaps Manuel Mantero has treated this theme with the greatest objectivity by putting things in perspective and reminding us of the differences between Panero's real Castile and Machado's ideal one, as between their religious conceptions.[17]

This kinship of expression, however, should be viewed more as an identity of chosen paths than as pure and simple influence – against which Mantero protests in the note cited. In effect, Machado provided not only for Panero, but for the other members of the Generation, an example of the concrete not encountered in the far more evasive existence practised by their teachers of the Generation of '27.

It is good to be shown the way. But each must take the road alone. This is the lesson in Panero's setting forth on the path that is to lead him to his definitive work.

Perhaps no one has comprehended the trajectory of this path more deeply than Dámaso Alonso in an essay to which we owe one of the stylistic keys to the poetry of Leopoldo Panero : the *arraigo* and its critical exegesis : "rooted in the earth, intertwined with the family, aspiring toward God."[18] Milestones of this road are the fragments of a great truncated poem "La estancia vacía", in which the overwhelming presence of memory reigns. But this poem, begun in the autumn of 1943 and published in the review *Escorial* in 1944, is preceded by some poems charged with the new-found voice of Panero : the nine-syllable lines dedicated to his brother who died in 1937 and the sonnet "Gallina ciega" also published in *Escorial* in 1941. The need for rootedness arises even in the leisurely contemplation of his family which the poet attempts to transform into poetry with proper names. Thus the first poem begins with these lines :

> A ti, Juan Panero, mi hermano,
> mi compañero y mucho más :
> a ti tan dulce y tan cercano;
> a ti para siempre jamás.[19]

> (To you, Juan Panero, my brother,
> my companion and much more :
> To you, so sweet and so near;
> to you forever and ever.)

Or the first tercet of the second, in which the compelling *ronda* once again invokes the beloved names :

[17]*Insula*, No. 193, p. 11.
[18]Panero, p. 12.
[19]Panero, p. 138.

86

Angel, Ricardo, Juan, abuelo, abuela,
nos tocan levemente, y sin palabras
nos hablan, nos tropiezan, les tocamos.[20]

(Angel, Ricardo, Juan, grandfather, grandmother,
touch us gently, and without words
they speak to us, meet us, we touch them.)

Perhaps in the light of these two poems we may concern ourselves with the fragments of "La estancia vacía". Before anything else, though, we must qualify its character of truncated poem of which we spoke a moment ago. Because the poet's death has left the poem in irremediable fragments, we may grasp perhaps the stylistic impact made in its day by the pursuance of a structure which offered itself as incomplete or more exactly as fragmentary in the image precisely of the memory from which the poem arose. Stylistically the mixture of meters seemingly underscores the poet's decision as to the best means of resolving the problem of continuity by offering us different metres and rhymes within the same poem, including even sonnets, as in the one beginning:

Es domingo quizá. Tiene fragancia
de domingo el pinar;....................[21]

(It is Sunday, perhaps. The pines
are giving off a Sunday fragrance;)

Or the one completing the book, "a sonnet of arboreal imagery, perhaps no more than an amplification of commentary on all we've written in this essay",[22] as Dámaso Alonso has called it, and which we cannot refrain from presenting in its entirety, since we agree with Alonso on the symbolic value it has for Panero's poetry:[23]

Señor, el viejo tronco se desgaja,
el recio amor nacido poco a poco
se rompe. El corazón, el pobre loco,
está llorando a solas en voz baja,

del viejo tronco haciendo pobre caja
mortal. Señor, la encina en huesos toco
deshecha entre mis manos, y Te invoco
en la santa vejez que resquebraja

su noble fuerza. Cada rama, en nudo,
era hermandad de savia y todas juntas
daban sombra feliz, orillas buenas.

[20]Panero, "A mis hermanos", p. 173.
[21]Panero, p. 88.
[22]Panero, p. 20.
[23]Panero, p. 21.

Señor, el hacha llama al tronco mudo,
golpe a golpe, y se llena de preguntas
el corazón del hombre donde suenas.[24]

(Dear Lord, this old tree is losing its branches,
the robust love that slowly came into being
is splintering. My heart, the poor demented thing,
is weeping all alone quietly,

making out of the old tree
a poor coffin. Dear Lord, I touch the oak,
bones fallen apart in my hands, and I invoke thy name
in the sacred old age which undermines

the strength of this noble tree. Each branch, connected,
formed a union of vital fluids and together the branches
provided joyous shade and spacious shores.

Dear Lord, the axe calls to the mute tree,
blow by blow, and the heart of the man
where thy presence is announced fills with questions.)

The seemingly truncated structure of "La estancia vacía" has a continuation in Spanish poetry – without it being possible to speak definitively of Panero's influence – in "Canto I" of Alfonso Costafreda's *Nuestra Elegía,* recipient of the Premio Boscán of 1949, in which Costafreda, in the same manner as Panero, includes poems which have an individualized existence, in the "Canto" which also mingles varied meters and rhyme schemes with unifying intent.[25]

The next book to appear was surely one of Leopoldo Panero's most successful. *Escrito a cada instante* gives space to poems written prior to "La estancia vacía" as the two already discussed among others. Little by little Leopoldo Panero's search marked out the path most to be his. Little by little he came to know himself. Intimately united though this new book may have been to "La estancia vacía", it springs, nevertheless, from a distinct formal purpose, and does not deal with the evocation of memory imposing the fragmentary vision which we have distinguished. Rather it treats of the search for God through the search for poetry, as noted by Dámaso Alonso in his double interpretation of the book's title, adding that "the reader (it seems) won't understand the poet well if he doesn't take this into account. The poet constantly deciphers the name of God, and constantly that name is hidden from him. And this eagerness, this glimpsing and losing sight of Him is the creating of poetry : his poetry. That is to say also that poetry is written at each instant, created at each instant. That the poet's existence is continuous creation : ceaseless conversion of his experience into poetry. Or : continuous reception of the divine surge".[26] Or to say it in the poet's own verses :

[24]Panero, p. 121.
[25]*Los Premios "Boscán" de poesía, 1949-1961* (Barcelona, 1964), pp. 12-14.
[26]Panero, p. 10.

                    Cada latido,
otra vez es más dulce, y otra y otra;
otra vez ciegamente desde dentro
va a pronunciar Su nombre.
Y otra vez se ensombrece el pensamiento
y la voz no le encuentra.
Dentro del pecho está.[27]

                    (Each heartbeat,
is again sweeter, and again and again;
once more blindly from within
it prepares to pronounce His name.
And once more the thought is lost in the shadow,
and the voice fails to find it.
It is left inside the breast.)

No wonder that at a time when Spanish poetry tends to offer books of only one current, in which the whole book is like one long poem – as in Luis Rosales' *La casa encendida* – Panero, faithful to his definition of poetry, offers us, on the other hand, books of more traditional cut, in which individualized poems – written at each instant – give us an account of the vision of the poet which may rest in God (as does the poem which we have mentioned and which gives the book its title). Written, whether in melancholy, or in the streets of his childhood or in an empty church, or in an old boat or in shipwrecks – where the persons evoked range from fellow poets, César Vallejo or Federico García Lorca, to acquaintances met in the street, the chestnut vendor Macaria, or those in familiar environs, the seamstress Dolores, or the poet's own sons. Not to mention the stuttering poem dedicated to Miguel de Cervantes, where we can find a last and lasting influence on Panero's poetry : that of César Vallejo.

Throughout the poems there breathes the veracious word of Leopoldo Panero, penetrating deeply into each of the themes treated. It now seems that Panero's years of searching which, as Luis Rosales affirms, "had not yet ceased. Strictly speaking, they never stopped",[28] established his domain most firmly. No wonder that after five years during which the poet seemed to take shelter in empty formalism, he should then return to the formula of this book in "Navidad en Caracas" (1955), "Desde el umbral de un sueño" (1959), "Siete poemas" (1959), "Romances y canciones" (1960) to end with the moving poem "Cándida puerta" (1960).

Between *Escrito a cada instante* and "Navidad en Caracas" the poet passes through an epoch marked instead by a formalism which seems to cloak a great aridity. The "Epístolas para mis amigos y enemigos" (1952–1953) were all composed in linked tercets – except perhaps the most outstanding, written for Eduardo Carranza. Addressing this to the Colombian poet inspired Panero to a majestic alexandrine, much more appropriate for the evocation of

[27]Panero, p. 133.
[28]*Cuadernos Hispanoamericanos*, Nos. 187-188, p. 70.

a Spanish American poet as well as stylistically more fitting. In the other letters as in the ones dedicated to the friends who had surrounded him, as in his "Carta perdida" to Pablo Neruda, Panero acknowledges the difficulties of a poetic formula : the sustained use of the tercet that ends by tiring the reader, although the poet may still show, throughout, absolute domination of form. If the tercets "are for grave matters", as Lope well knew in his "Arte nuevo de hacer comedias", and Panero utilized them for just this reason, i.e., to empty his generous heart in a series of deep and fixed preoccupations, the end products of friendship or disillusion, the sustained torrent of the tercets does not seem the most expressive mode for a contemporary writer.

The epistle dedicated to Neruda, nevertheless, stands out in Panero's work almost as though it were a complete book; it has given rise to a polemic that often has had nothing to do with literature. Antonio Tovar could affirm : "Once again it is opportune to reflect on Leopoldo Panero's duel with the great Chilean poet, and thus help to explain the *Canto personal* which, objectively viewed, seems to me one of the summits of Panero's poetry, if not in intensity, then in force."[29] No criticism could be more just, principally for two reasons : because of the enormous importance Neruda has had in Spanish poetry, and because of the quixotic element in Panero's gesture.

Let us begin by saying that in our opinion the most eminent voice in Hispanic poetry today is Neruda's. For the very excellence which that voice attains, Panero's attempt seems all the more valiant and valuable. When viewed from the only possible perspective in judging poetry : " . . . then Panero's *Canto* is not, all things considered, a doctrinal book, nor a pamphlet, or a political discourse, but – and there lies the heart of the matter – precisely a poetic work",[30] as Eugenio de Nora has reminded us.

In the same essay, Nora points out Leopoldo Panero's moral intent in writing this book. The moral tone – not political, as Nora opportunely specifies – is the one Panero shares with the members of a generation who knew how to make, while Panero was attacking some controversial aspects of Neruda,[31] one of the most vibrant confessions of what they initially stood for.

Possibly Neruda's *Canto general* and Panero's *Canto personal* have a weakness in common : those moments when both writers forget their respective *tones* and thus contradict the purpose their poems meant to serve. In the case of Neruda it is evident that the work, which is in almost every particular the essence of a collective voice – *Canto general*, the title speaks for itself – fails structurally to support the poet's excessively personal reaction to people or events. The opposite occurs in the case of Panero : in a poem adhering to the tenets of individualism – or *personalism* as Unamuno would have categorized it – a nadir is plumbed when the poet, seduced by the dialectics of the book he meant to attack, passed imperceptibly from his accustomed first person singular to the first person plural.

In the Panerian *yo* we have authentic emotion, persuasive confession, while his *nosotros* inevitably compels him to grope for a collective pretext, defined in terms of political compromise clashing with his entire work and his entire life.

[29]*Ibid.*, p. 131.
[30]*Insula*, No. 193, p. 10.
[31]*Ibid.*, enumerated by Nora.

Yet we must reiterate that these contradictions, which would be grave in the sphere of thought, are much less so when we analyze the works of Neruda and Panero in their function as poetry, the sole level on which analysis should be maintained. In the case of Panero, our only possible conclusion would be that there is less intensity in those moments when he does not speak in the tone of his generation which, in the remainder of his work, he so well represents.

If this poetic altercation with Neruda produced a dozen controversial verses, his last contacts with Spanish America, in 1955, when he visits Venezuela and other countries, restore his better voice, associated – after the wasteland years – with his most authentic poetic direction. What is strange is that the first poem, "Navidad en Caracas", retains the epistolary structure the poet has come to use in his last years. But – as occurred in the case of the letter dedicated to Carranza – here also the ambiance of Spanish America which has always supported, in harmony with its nature and its soul, a more ample metre for poetry in the Castilian tongue as Unamuno knew so well, this presence diminishes the tercet's sorcery over Panero's speaking and gives him a free verse in which the frequent invocations to Manuel Felipe Rugeles, to whom the poem is dedicated, flow with greater naturalness. From this juncture, Panero's poetry, without further vacilation, rediscovers the lost vein of his preceding books up to *Escrito a cada instante* and surges toward the book's last magnificent poems : "Callada canción" and "Cándida puerta". This last poem perhaps conveys the essence of Panerian poetry in its search for a sincere identity. The beginning and the end of this poem evoke simply a bakery door :

> Cuando la madrugada baja al pueblo
> y cubre los tejados fina escarcha,
> sólo el que amasa, vela; y se oye el cálido
> rumor de su trabajo desde el húmedo
> corazón de la noche...............................
> ....
> ¡Oh arañada tahona, puerta tibia,
> única casa viva en todo el orbe,
> radiante vecindad, jara aromosa,
> que arde y que toca el pan con gracia súbita.
> Señor, Señor, de tu presencia hablo,
> ¡acoge la intemperie de mi alma
> y el montón de mis huesos, para heñirlos
> a la vida de nuevo, y que, en mi mano,
> céntimo de tahona el verso sea
> como es todo mi ser dádiva tuya ![32]

> (When dawn descends on the town,
> and a light frost covers the rooftops,
> the dough-mixer alone stands vigil; and the warm
> sounds of his work
> rise out of the night's humid heart . . .

[32]Panero, pp. 443 and 448.

Oh, web-spun bake-shop, warm doorway,
vibrant abode, unique the world around,
radiant community, fragrant rockrose,
that glows, touching the bread with quickening grace.
Dear Lord, I am speaking of thy presence :
Take from me the turbulence surrounding my soul
and these heaped-up bones, and knead them
into renewed life, and let this poem, from my hand,
be acceptable in exchange for bread
as is my whole being your gift to me.)

    While the above was the last poem of Leopoldo Panero to be gathered into the edition of his complete works, we now have, thanks to his son Juan Luis, a series of the poet's unedited poems, ending with the one written on the very morning of the day of his death. This final poem, in its sadly incomplete form, may perhaps epitomize for us the general tendency of Panero's poetry as well as the forces which shape the poetic expression of the entire Spanish Generation of 1936 : a kind of tenacious return to the real – even in poems such as "Cándida puerta" where a symbolic aura mingles with elements of actuality. This last poem does not require any exegesis. For that reason, it may serve as a climax to this paper.

    ... Como en los perros,
tocados por su amo,
vaga todo lo amigo de la tierra,
así quisiera mi palabra :
simple,
parada en las pupilas,
y con errantes sílabas de niño.

Improvisar el mundo,
y todo lo diáfano del mundo,
con la fecha encontrada en el rocío
y con el tibio soplo de la mano ...

Porque lo que vale es lo real
escrito con el vaho de lo real,
y con el poso aéreo
del corazón que late llamado por su dueño,
leve,
muy levemente,
oh, poema.[33]

(... As with dogs,
touched by their master,

---

[33]*Cuadernos Hispanoamericanos*, Nos. 187-188, pp. 32-33.

all that is friendly on earth wanders aimlessly,
this I would wish for my word :
simple,
imprinted on the eyes,
and with the child's errant syllables.

To improvise the world,
and all that is diaphanous,
with today's date found on the dew
and with the hand's warm breeze . . .

Because what counts is the real
written with the mist of the real,
and with the airy sediment
of the pulsating heart that is summoned gently
very gently
by its master,
oh, poem.)

Pablo Neruda and the Renewal
of Spanish Poetry During the Thirties*

JUAN CANO-BALLESTA

The literary and artistic climate of the years of the Spanish Republic (1931–1939), so restless and enmeshed in the numerous manifestos, poetry magazines, and avant-garde movements, is decisively marked in the field of lyric poetry by the esthetic conceptions of the great figures of the so-called Generation of 1927 and their already-established masters of the early 20th century. What has not been sufficiently recognized however is the influence and the role played by others who, although minor figures at the time, deserve to be taken very much into account because they contributed an innovating, and at times revolutionary, element. Very significant in this respect is the Chilean poet Pablo Neruda, whose friendship with several poets of the then-emerging young generation was in many aspects decisive for them, and whose presence in Madrid, where he was admired by many and attacked by some, deserves to be studied for a proper understanding of the movement of forces, in its interesting complexity, which has made possible the great flowering of Spanish poetry in recent decades.

Neruda's arrival in Madrid was a fertile encounter within the Hispanic literary world, an event comparable in many respects to Rubén Darío's visit some four decades before. Yet the Spanish literary scene was quite different. The Chilean diplomat did not now have to confront the literary impoverishment and spiritual exhaustion of the 1890's, but rather a great scientific, literary, and poetic flowering, an intense intellectual and artistic life. Neruda's poetry dazzled and exasperated the literary circles of Madrid where the prestige of the strophe-cultivators, of the creators of the "precise word," and of intellectual poetry was still forceful enough to affect younger poets like the Panero brothers, Miguel Hernández, Luis Rosales and Luis Felipe Vivanco, and to indicate the path for their initial steps. This despite the literary works of surrealist inspiration

*This article attempts to give a new and more ambitious approach to the talk I gave at the symposium on "The Generation of 1936", November 12, 1967, at Syracuse University, and which was subsequently published in *Symposium*, XXII (1968), 123-31. I am grateful to the editor of *La Torre* for permission to reproduce a couple of pages from my article "Miguel Hernández y su amistad con Pablo Neruda (Crisis estética e ideológica a la luz de unos documentos)", *La Torre*, no. 60 (summer, 1968). These added pages make it possible to offer a more complete study of the subject announced in the title. [Translation is by D.P.T.]

and torrential style which had been written (let us recall the Lorca of *Poeta en Nueva York* and Vicente Aleixandre). The presence of a corrosive element and ferment like that of Neruda's *Residencia* enriched the creative possibilities by providing a powerful renovating ingredient. In turn Neruda received in Madrid the lesson of control which his fluvial and volcanic "New World romanticism" so badly needed; he learned to fuse (as he himself confessed in a talk in 1939), "mystery with exactness, classicism with passion".[1] At the same time his triumph in the capital city with the help of García Lorca, then the most popular poet, had the effect of giving the Chilean writer a definitive standing in both continents.

Having sailed from Buenos Aires, Neruda arrived as the Chilean consul in Barcelona in May, 1934, from where he began to come into contact with the poets and writers of the Spanish capital. On December 6, 1934, he delivered a recital-lecture at the University of Madrid, where he was introduced by Federico García Lorca who synthesized in his remarks what must have excited the Spanish public most : lyricism of the unfamiliar and the aberrant which dares to break molds, which has no fear of sentimental effusion, which is capable of intense enthusiasm and tears, and which inundates like a naked elemental force :

> I advise you to be prepared to hear one of those authentic poets who have their senses masterly attuned to a world which is not ours and which few people perceive . . . A poet full of mysterious voices which fortunately he himself has not learned to decipher; a real man who already knows that the bulrush and the swallow are more eternal than the hard cheek of a statue . . . But not all these poets have a New World tone. Many seem to be Spanish and others bring out foreign notes (especially French) in their voices. But not the great poets. In the great ones, the broad, romantic, harsh, aberrant, mysterious light of the New World crackles. Blocks on the verge of sinking, poems balanced over the abyss on a spider's thread, a smile that reminds us slightly of the jaguar, a large hairy hand delicately playing with a small lace handkerchief. These poets express the impudent tone of the great Spanish language of the New World inhabitants, a language closely linked to the sources of our classics, a poetry which holds no shame in breaking molds, which has no fear of the ridiculous, and which bursts out crying in the middle of the street.[2]

Anyone reading García Lorca's letters of a few years before 1934 dealing with literary themes will be surprised by the truly obsessive insistence with which he speaks of "renunciation" as a poetic attitude. The ghost of sentimentalism and

[1]The speech, given at the Teatro Mitre of Montevideo before the "Agrupación de Intelectuales, Artistas, Periodistas y Escritores" on March 24, 1939, was published under the title "España no ha muerto" and includes the following in the passage to which I referred: "I understood then that our New-World romanticism, our fluvial and volcanic construction, was in need of that primary alliance – fusing mystery with exactness, classicism with passion, the past with future prospects – which I saw almost accomplished in Spain before this terrible war began." Emilio Oribe, Juan Marinello, and Pablo Neruda, *Neruda entre nosotros* (Montevideo, 1939), p. 38.
[2]Pablo Neruda, *Selección* (Santiago de Chile, 1943), pp. 305-06.

romantic verbosity haunts him : "true poetry which is love, effort, and renunciation" . . . "I love the human voice. The human voice alone impoverished by love" . . . "the wretched and divine voice." And to remove all doubt, he concludes : "Let us now say it. May God free us from the tropics (pray for me)."[3] A dread of spontaneity and romantic effusion! A worship of control and renunciation! This was the Lorquian ideal. The taste being imposed during the years of the Spanish Republic bore precisely the opposite sign : the start of an unrestrained deluge, as in Nature.

To these efforts, Neruda did nothing but provide a powerful impulse after finally taking up residence in Madrid in February, 1935. If on his first visit in 1927 he had found the literary world impervious to his innovating experiments, on his second trip in 1934 he was able to count on "a brilliant fraternity of talents". The previously uncomprehended poet felt recognized and admired for the first time in his life – as he himself emphasizes; his friends and the literary critics of Madrid revealed to him the intimate organic structure of his work and they obligated him to be fully conscious of his art :

> When I stepped off the train, only one person was waiting for me, a bouquet of flowers in his hand : it was Federico. Few poets have been treated as I was in Spain. I found a brilliant fraternity of talents and a thorough familiarity with my work. Martyred for so many years by the public's incomprehension, by insults, and by malicious indifference – the drama of all authentic poets in our countries – I now felt happy.[4]

The sincere admiration and friendship surrounding him materialized in an homage-pamphlet (published by Editorial Plutardo), which contains three "Cantos materiales" from *Residencia en la tierra* dedicated to him by Spanish poets, and in which attention is again drawn to Neruda's extremely personal and innovative poetry. The contributors' names appear by generation : the established poets are in the first group, and in the second the younger poets all join the circle of friends and admirers. The dedication reads as follows :

> Chile has sent to Spain the great poet Pablo Neruda, whose visible creative energy, in full control of its poetic destiny, is producing very individual works, to the honor of the Spanish language. We, as poets and admirers of the young and renowned Spanish-American writer, upon publishing these unprinted poems – the latest examples of his magnificent poetry – do no more than stress his extraordinary personality, and his unquestionable literary stature. In reiterating our cordial welcome to him on this occasion, the following Spanish poets are pleased to make public once again their admiration for a work which indisputably constitutes one of the most authentic poetic realities in the Spanish language :

[3]Federico García Lorca's letter from Granada of September 9, 1926, to Jorge Guillén ("Ateneo", Valladolid), reproduced in Jorge Guillén, *Federico en persona (Semblanza y epistolario)*, (Buenos Aires, 1959).
[4]Alfredo Cardona Peña, *Pablo Neruda y otros ensayos* (México, 1955), pp. 30-31.

RAFAEL ALBERTI, VICENTE ALEIXANDRE, MANUEL ALTOLAGUIRRE, LUIS CERNUDA, GERARDO DIEGO, LEON FELIPE, FEDERICO GARCIA LORCA, JORGE GUILLEN, PEDRO SALINAS.

MIGUEL HERNANDEZ, JOSE A. MUNOZ ROJAS, LEOPOLDO Y JUAN PANERO, LUIS ROSALES, ARTURO SERRANO PLAJA, LUIS FELIPE VIVANCO.[5]

With his *Residencia en la tierra* Neruda offered what many young poets were impatiently seeking as they became conscious of themselves and as they began to feel so distinct from their predecessors : a new sensibility. Neruda was an esthetic revolutionary. His impetuous primitive force shatters the established forms. Poetic feeling flows freely and is valued more highly than the conscious development of style. Like many of his young contemporaries who were capable of giving poetic fullness to traditional forms, Miguel Hernández found them excessively restricted and felt paralyzed by the formidable prestige and authority of the previous generation of poets. Thanks to his provocative manifestos on "impure poetry", Neruda strongly affected the young poets, almost all of whom were beginning to publish some of their poems in *Caballo verde para la poesía* and who were being drawn to the Chilean consul. It is true – as Emir Rodríguez Monegal observes, recalling the parallel which we mentioned before – that "Darío never found in Spain the kind of formidable, tenacious and eloquent enmity as that which Juan Ramón Jiménez expressed for Neruda and which is the basis of the extraordinary and unjust poetic caricature found in *Españoles de tres mundos*".[6] Juan Ramón Jiménez's nervousness and alarm are precisely an eloquent testimony that he considered his position dangerously threatened as the supreme pontiff of the muses. Neruda became the younger poet's older brother and thus gradually set himself up as an anti-Juan-Ramón.

This fact has not sufficiently been taken into account. Luis Rosales has noted it and speaks of a "conspiracy of silence" with respect to the battle Neruda waged in Madrid against pure poetry. He has been disregarded. But the truth is that, amid the disquiet and effervescence of divergent esthetic conceptions dominant during those years in Madrid, a large number of young poets, imbued with the avant-garde spirit, saw in Pablo Neruda a likely leader in this polemic. Rosales recalls the impact produced by Neruda's manifesto placed on the first page of *Caballo verde* : "Those of us who lived through it will not forget. Neruda's manifesto was extraordinarily accurate; to those of us then young poets, it confirmed our convictions and it opened unimagined perspectives before us. We had to create an impure poetry, like a suit of clothes, like a human body, with food stains and shameful gestures, with wrinkles, observations, dreams, vigils, prophesies . . . "[7]

---

[5] Pablo Neruda, *Selección* (Santiago de Chile, 1943), p. 317.
[6] Emir Rodríguez Monegal, "Darío y Neruda : un paralelo imposible", *La Torre*, XV (no. 55-56; January-June, 1967), p. 103.
[7] Luis Rosales, "Leopoldo Panero hacia un nuevo humanismo", *Cuadernos Hispanoamericanos*, no. 187-188 (July-August, 1965), p. 65.

From his Olympian retreat, Juan Ramón Jiménez hurled his thunderbolts against the rebels. His attitude towards Neruda's poetry could not be more definitive :

> I have always considered Pablo Neruda ... a great Poet, a great bad poet, a magnificent poet of disorganization; the talented poet who has not understood nor utilized his natural gifts ...
>
> Neruda has exploited, and has still to exploit, his mine; he has the unusual intuition, the strange searching, the fatal discovery, the native genius of the poet; he has neither a personal accent nor a full critical faculty. He possesses a reservoir of all that he has encountered in his world, something resembling a rubbish dump, or even a dungheap sometimes, where a stone, a flower, an as yet uncorroded piece of metal, all still beautiful, have come to rest amid the leftovers, the waste, and the junk. He finds the rose, the diamond, the gold, but not the representative and transforming word.[8]

Juan Ramón was nonetheless aware that a void was opening up around him. When the magazine *Nueva Poesía,* published by Juan Ruiz Peña and Luis Pérez Infante at the same time as *Caballo verde para la poesía* (that is, in the fall of 1935), appeared with a provocative manifesto and a list of the five or six best Spanish poets which omitted the name of Antonio Machado, it was fiercely attacked by the Madrid critics. It was already behind the times. Its dominant esthetic ideas were no longer in force in the capital. It was attacked for cultivating a type of poetry after the manner of Paul Valéry. The only person to come to its defense was Juan Ramón Jiménez. Juan Ruiz Peña accurately observes : "Almost all of the Spanish public interested in poetry was divided between Juan Ramón and Neruda, while Antonio Machado, a solitary diamond, was a brilliant gleam in the shadow, foretelling the poetry of the future."[9]

Miguel Hernández – the most daring and revolutionary poet of his group, for which reason he requires special attention – becomes precisely the admirer and vociferous spokesman of the new esthetic represented by Neruda. There is a critical review of his on Neruda's *Residencia en la tierra;* it has occasionally been alluded to, but never carefully studied. It reveals a perspicacious critic capable of grasping essential aspects of Neruda's poetry and feeling the pulse of the prevalent literary tastes in the Madrid of 1935 which, tired of certain abuses of intellectual and purist poetry, vibrated in all directions in search of more breathable horizons. Miguel Hernández's criticism has the distinction of being an acute diagnosis of this particular time and an outcry in favor of an esthetic renewal :

> I need to communicate the enthusiasm affecting me since I read *Residencia en la tierra.* I feel like throwing handfuls of sand in my eyes,

---

[8]Juan Ramón Jiménez, *Españoles de tres mundos* (Madrid, 1960), pp. 218-220.
[9]Juan Ruiz Peña, "Historia de una amistad (Leopoldo Panero y yo)", *Cuadernos Hispanoamericanos,* no. 187-188 (July-August, 1965), p. 195.

letting my fingers get caught in closing doors, clambering up to the very top of the tallest and most rugged pine tree. It would be the most effective way of expressing the violent admiration stirred in me by a poet of these gigantic dimensions . . .

There are poets whose voices fit in a thimble, in a three-syllable line; they should not spread out in an Alexandrine. It is like those wide rivers that carry no water.

Pablo Neruda's voice is an oceanic clamor which cannot be contained, a lament too primitive and powerful to permit rhetorical confinements. We are hearing the virgin voice of the man who drags his leonine instincts over the earth; it is a roar; and no one tries to restrain a roar. Look in others for the subjection to what is officially called form. In him things are given as in the Bible and the ocean : freely and grandiosely.[10]

Published in the literary section of *El Sol,* a Madrid daily of wide circulation, this review, the only one known to have been written by Miguel Hernández, is a forceful announcement of the presence of a man and of the collapse of an esthetic. Hernández is fully conscious of it when he states : "He comes to belittle and tear down things that up to now were considered imposing and durable." The self-taught poet who had begun his creative work in heroic octaves and flawless sonnets perceives that what he had long intuited and dreamed has been accomplished by a prestigious poet : to give free rein to his lyrical feeling, to release them from restraints and chains. It is what he repeats almost obsessively in a letter to Juan Guerrero : "I know once and for all that restraints of any kind cannot be placed on the lyric poem."

Once certain idols had been toppled, the literary atmosphere was renewed with growing speed and intensity. The young poets began to speak unabashedly from the heart. In opposition to intellectual poetry, which had been made fashionable by the mature Juan Ramón Jiménez and his distinguished disciples Jorge Guillén and Pedro Salinas, Pablo Neruda is seen as the guide for a type of poetry that issues freely from the heart. And this is another of the innovations that the young poet-turned-critic discovers :

I say that Pablo Neruda approaches things with his heart, not with his head. He surrounds objects with insignias of the heart, and he kneels in their presence considering them as lost, even though they remain in his power . . .

This is the kind of poetry I prefer, because it leaves and enters the heart directly. I detest purely intellectual poetic games. I love the manifestations of the blood and not those of reason, which ruins everything with its intellectualizing ice.

After two decades of careful artistry and intense pruning – or, as García Lorca said, "renunciation" – poetry threatened to lose its spontaneity, ingenuousness and freshness. The return to a more romantic attitude relied on the sympathy

[10]Folletones de *El Sol,* (Madrid, January 2, 1936).

of young people. Miguel Hernández approached life to extract from it force, inspiration, authenticity, motifs, and to mold them with astonishing immediacy in the poem. In a word, he openly gave in to the "heresy of feeling" (to use Baudelaire's expression). He gathers together his anguish, pain and joys in order to turn them into poetic substance : love passion, the grief of incomprehension, the anguished premonition that the "carnivorous knife" menaced his life, his inner world inhabited by anxieties and tragic spectres; and all of this unblushingly put into form by a person apparently unafraid of exposing his intimate being. Hernández sings of these things in passionate dramatic tones, in expressions of overwhelming intensity. All this was without question unusual prior to that time.

The return to the theme of the heart finds firm support in the restoration of romantic elements demanded by Pablo Neruda in the first issue of *Caballo verde* :

> And let us never forget melancholy and worn-out sentimentalism, those impure but perfect products that possess a forgotten marvellous quality, left behind by the frenzy over the printed word : moonlight, the swan at twilight, "dear sweetheart", are no doubt basic and indispensable to poetry. He who runs from bad taste falls into ice.[11]

Miguel Hernández – to cite the most outstanding example – had not been ashamed to translate his intimate love experiences into poems long before he knew Neruda. The latter had come very opportunely to swell the ranks of a movement and he succeeded with prestige and authority in formulating ideas which several young poets of the Spanish capital felt deeply during those years. Luis Rosales, with several unpublished love sonnets in his pocket, felt scorned by the already-established poets like Rafael Alberti, who spoke contemptuously of those who were writing "verses to their sweethearts". Germán Bleiberg, another member of the group, published his *Sonetos amorosos* in 1936, a book marked by an emphasis on feeling (although too often timidly expressed) and highly charged with delicate melancholy in the manner of Garcilaso.

But let us not be deceived. Although Salinas wrote books on love like *La voz a ti debida* (1933) or *Razón de amor* (1936), he never abandoned his conceptual, rather abstract, intellectual tone, so remote from the intense emotion and concreteness of the love sonnets of a Miguel Hernández. And there is no doubt that the only book comparable in this respect is Neruda's *Veinte poemas de amor y una canción desesperada,* which had had many authorized and pirated editions since 1932 both in Buenos Aires and Madrid, and which is significant as an evident reinforcement of the new developments. Echoes of this book are suggested at least in several poems of Hernández', for whom love, as for Neruda, is carnal, sensual and passionate, and is in marked contrast to Salinas' characteristic treatment of the theme.

If we compare some of the poems written in those years by the young poets who joined in the homage to Neruda and who contributed later to *Caballo verde,* we are particularly struck by an avant-garde, experimental posture. Leopoldo Panero published a very revealing poem "Por el centro del día" in the first issue.

[11]Pablo Neruda, *Obras completas* (Buenos Aires, 1962), p. 1823.

We see there very little of the later Panero. He gives us the style of a moment of effervescence, of experimentation, more than a projection of himself. There is a little of Neruda and much of Aleixandre, but in particular there is an obsessive desire to be up-to-date, to contribute something new, or to join the latest vanguard :

¡Qué dulce tu figura labrada en el misterio !
Si tu mano se abre las margaritas flotan sobre el campo ligero.
Si tu pecho increíble suspira y se acongoja parece que es la muerte como
    un cáliz de espuma y de jilgueros verdes.
¡Ah ! mujer aceptada por mi llanto sin fondo.
Porque perderte sería como apretar un ruiseñor con las manos llenas de
    ríos verdes y de ciudades,
y como ir hundiendo tristemente los labios sobre un astro de palabras
    puras.

....

¡Ah ! mujer aceptada por mi llanto sin fondo.
Tu carne tiene el gracioso color del pan y de la lágrima,
y tu cuerpo se diviniza como una nube solitaria sorprendida por la aurora.
El mar vuelve sobre la playa
y arrebata la arena trémula y las conchas donde han dormido las primeras
    violetas de marzo.
Parece que el amor huye siempre más lejos y su presencia luminosa
    parece como la sombra de un deseo.[12]

(How sweet your countenance wrought in mystery !
If your hand opens, daisies float gently over the fields.
If your extraordinary breast, overcome by anguish, gives off a sigh, it
    seems that death is like a chalice filled with foam and green linnets.
Ah, woman sheltered in the abyss of my grief.
Because losing you would be to press a nightingale in my hands that are
    filled with green rivers and with cities,
and slowly and sadly to plunge my lips around a star of pure words.

....

Ah, woman sheltered in the abyss of my grief.
Your flesh has the pleasing color of bread and tears,
and your body is suddenly divine like a solitary cloud surprised by dawn.
The ocean comes back over the beach
and passionately seizes the trembling sand and the conches where the first
    violets of March lay dormant.
Love seems to have flown to more distant lands ; its luminous presence is
    only the shadow of a longing.)

[12]Cf. *Cuadernos Hispanoamericanos*, no. 187-188 (July-August, 1965), p. 62.

There is no unifying structure in this somewhat long poem but rather a succession of impressions. Written in the period of poetic manifestos, the poem is one in which the personal is replaced by a rhetoric of originality. It is a moment of extreme innovating tension, of the battle against pure poetry in which Pablo Neruda appears on the scene with his prestige precisely to tip the scales – much to Juan Ramón Jiménez' regret – in favour of the young poets.

It is of some interest to recall an episode of the personal and poetic bonds between Neruda and the young writers of 1935, who as enthusiasts joined in the homage to him, because twenty years later there was to be conflict and a dramatic severing of these bonds upon the appearance of Neruda's *Canto general*. Leopoldo Panero composed a long poem which he entitled *Canto personal (Carta perdida a Pablo Neruda)*. The work contains a prologue by Dionisio Ridruejo, another poet and literary companion, in which, speaking on behalf of Luis Rosales and Luis Felipe Vivanco, he moves away from the poetry, ideology and over-all attitude of Neruda's *Canto*.

Panero upbraids him for his sensationalistic, noisy and strident voice, and for his radical change from estheticism to the poetry of hatred :

> Tu estético Caballo de Esmeralda
> para la Poesía, qué distante;
> hoy eres un puñal contra la espalda,
> Pablo : con tus palabras te derrotas
> enteramente solo; y con tu acento
> de tempestad no empujas las gaviotas.

> (Your esthetic Emerald Horse
> for Poetry, how far away it is;
> today you are a knife in the back,
> Pablo : with your words you alone
> bring ruin upon yourself; upon the whirlwind
> in your voice, the seagulls do not take wing.)

His tone turns emotional, combative, insulting :

> El que hace profesión (y de ella vive)
> de obrero de palabras . . .

> (The one who makes his profession – and makes his living
> from it – as a workman of words . . .)

Panero accuses Neruda of being "lost in the absolute" in his fight for a humanitarian abstraction, a remote future, a communist paradise, when it would be more humane to help the hungry neighbor at our side :

> No caridad total y en lontananza
> (que ésa sólo es de Dios), sino vecina
> y personal, con vaho de esperanza.[13]

[13]Leopoldo Panero, *Poesía (1932–1960)* (Madrid, 1963), pp. 339, 303, 304, 302, and 303 respectively.

(Not universal and inaccessible charity
– that belongs only to God – but one that is
close by and personal, with a glimmer of hope.)

With this break, four important poets of the generation, Pablo Neruda's admirers through the Thirties, split off – for reasons more ideological than esthetic – from the person who earlier had been a master and an admired and respected poet. Just the contrary occurred with Miguel Hernández, in whom Neruda's poetry took root and endured all his life in the form of an intense friendship and in similar poems of social commitment.

There remains finally another important aspect in which the presence of the Chilean diplomat served as the innovating impulse and here again Miguel Hernández was the most revolutionary poet of his group. In the difficult years of the economic crisis and in the disorganized milieu of the Spanish Republic, writers were becoming aware of their responsibility. During the years of Primo de Rivera's dictatorship the immediate world had its order, and the poet could concentrate his efforts on his artistic work and create his own serene, illuminated poetic world or his mythical world of dreaming gypsies. All this was brought down by the thrust of reality which, during the Republic, did not permit the writer to create his own world but rather forced him to live and sing in the threatened public world. The shifting ground begins to tremble under the writer's feet. The changing political situation ushers forth an unsuspected horizon of opportunities but with it also a great insecurity. In an article published in *La Prensa* of Buenos Aires on the 20th of September, 1931, Ramiro de Maeztu notes how the writers who had dedicated their existence to the refinement of style, those proclaiming that "to associate a noun with an adjective for the first time was the loftiest exploit to which a writer could aspire", in the atmosphere of the Spanish Republic "began to be in the eyes of most people, more than anything else, evangelists of the revolution". The social and artistic climate changes profoundly. The estheticist tendency, the faith in "the absolute autonomy of art" (in Gautier's words) finally loses all prestige. In January, 1935, Maeztu cites expressions current in literary circles, like the following two of Domenico Guilliotti : "Pure poet is equivalent to imbecile; poet, simply put, is equivalent to hero." "At best, the pure poet is an esthete . . . but at worst, he is a swine."[14]

The revolution of 1934 among Asturian miners was sufficient to inflame and to project this uneasiness into literary works of social commitment and protest. Rafael Alberti and León Felipe had already turned in that direction some years before. Miguel Hernández, receptive to all the incitements found in abundance in the national capital, understood the potential function of poetry as a social mission, undertaking to create that "prophetic poetry" of which he had spoken several years before and whose mission it was "to propagate feelings" and "to vivify lives".

In the third issue of *Caballo verde* (December, 1935), the Chilean poet expressed the necessity which may force a poet under the pressure of certain

---

[14]Cf. *ABC,* (January 13, 1935). Ramiro de Maeztu, *Las letras y la vida en la España de entreguerras* (Madrid, 1958), pp. 40-41, 46, 63.

circumstances to "vilify himself" with such themes as haste, war, destruction :

> When time with its daily decisive flash eats away at us, and solid attitudes, confidences and blind faith are plunged into ruin, and the poet's loftiness tends to descend, spat out like the most forlorn mother-of-pearl, we wonder if the hour has not arrived to vilify ourselves, the painful hour to consider how man survives on a primitive level, biting and scratching, fending selfishly for himself. And how teeth, fingernails and the branches of the ferocious tree of hate make their way into the house of poetry.[15]

This is precisely what Miguel Hernández does in numerous poems beginning in 1935 : men in the claws of hate, the desire to destroy, the bitterness of grief, hunger, prisons, are all converted into socially-oriented poetic themes. There is a common attitude toward poetry and life, to which Miguel Hernández clings under the spell of his poetic instinct, and which Neruda formulates theoretically in his manifesto.

In this particular case, although Neruda's poetic doctrine figured importantly at the center of the literary scene, I think that it was rather Raúl Gonzáles Tuñon who, with the living example of his book *La rosa blindada* (*Homenaje a la Insurrección de Asturias y otros poemas revolucionarios*), provided Hernández with the definitive push towards the poetry of political harangue. Stimulated by this work, M. Hernández set about creating revolutionary literature and produced socially-committed poetry that is bespattered with the impurities of the moment and historical circumstance. This took place in 1935, precisely with the subject of a miners' revolt in *Los hijos de la piedra* (*Drama del monte y sus jornaleros*). About this time (undoubtedly in 1935, since his state of mind was identical to the one expressed in a letter to Juan Guerrero of April of the same year), he also wrote the poem "Sonreídme", an intense revolutionary and anticlerical *canto* :

> Me libré de los templos, sonreídme,
> donde me consumía con tristeza de lámpara
> encerrado en el poco aire de los sagrarios;
> salté al monte donde procedo,
> a las viñas donde halla tanta hermana mi sangre,
> a vuestra compañía de relativo barro . . .
> Ya relampaguean
> las hachas y las hoces con su metal crispado,
> ya truenan los martillos y los mazos
> sobre los pensamientos de los que nos han hecho
> burros de carga y bueyes de labor.
> Salta el capitalista de su cochino lujo,
> huyen los arzobispos de sus mitras obscenas,
> los notarios y los registradores de la propiedad
> caen aplastados bajo furiosos protocolos,
> los curas se deciden a ser hombres,

---

[15]Pablo Neruda, *Obras completas* (Buenos Aires, 1962), pp. 1823-24.

y abierta ya la jaula donde actúa de león
queda el oro en la más espantosa miseria.[16]

(I got free of the temples (smile upon me),
where I was being consumed by lamplight sadness
enclosed in the stifling air of the sanctuaries;
I ran off to the wooded hills where I was born,
to the vineyards where my blood finds so many kinfolk,
to your companionship of relative clay . . .
                    Our axes and sickles
– their metal straining – have begun to sparkle,
our hammers and mallets are thundering down
on the thoughts of those who have made us into
pack-donkeys and ploughing oxen.
The capitalist jumps from his filthy luxury,
the archbishops flee from their obscene miters,
notaries and deed recorders
are crushed under the fury of protocols,
priests decide to be men;
and left in the sprung-open cage where it performs
like a lion is gold in the most hideous misery.)

Miguel Hernández takes wing and in this instance he anticipates his master in enthusiasm for revolutionary poetry. Pablo Neruda would decide to write poems of this type only in July of 1936, after hearing the first shots of the Civil War from his "house of the flowers" in Madrid. Hernández, the timid self-taught poet, under the pressure of circumstances, began to make accessible to Spanish poetry paths barely traveled and in many respects new, cultivating a social poetry in epico-lyrical rhythms, a committed poetry, intensely linked to the historical moment. He created such outstanding social poems with such intense feeling that, as José Luis Cano says, "if we wanted to symbolize Spanish social poetry in a single name, we would have to submit the name of Miguel Hernández".[17]

In the creation of social poetry, written before the start of the Civil War, Pablo Neruda's presence was very slight in the artistic realm, but in the human and political realms it was overwhelming. If the Chilean consul inspired and spurred the young poets toward a new type of poetry, if he moved others like Miguel Hernández toward an ideology from which revolutionary poetry fell like a ripe fruit, we cannot affirm the same with respect to the established and mature poets. It is true (as Rodríguez Monegal observes) that Neruda knew "the comradeship of García Lorca and Alberti, of Vicente Aleixandre and Manuel Altolaguirre, around the year 1934. But comradeship, not discipleship. In many respects the Spanish poets whose ranks he joined in Republican Spain preceded and even marked with their work certain political directions that Neruda's work would take".[18] It is evident that the Chilean poet's evolution toward a committed

[16]Miguel Hernández, *Obras completas* (Buenos Aires, 1960), p. 259.
[17]*Insula*, no. 226 (September 1965).
[18]Emir Rodríguez Monegal, p. 103 (see note 6, above).

poetry would be difficult to explain without Alberti, something which Neruda himself has admitted.

At any rate Pablo Neruda was an indispensable ingredient in the literary life of those years in Madrid. In whatever artistic commemoration or poetic function, he was present as an integral part of the bustling cultural life of the national capital. Whether it was a celebration in honor of a literary prize or the Book Festival of May, 1936, the banquet honoring the poet Cernuda or the reception for a Catalonian painter, Neruda never failed to appear. Jorge Guillén evokes one of these tumultuous reunions:

> What a surprising number of poets. They are brought together by affinities not entirely elective. But, how different they really are. Here they all are – the 20th of April, 1936 – at the dinner honoring Luis Cernuda. The person offering the words of homage is García Lorca; no one else would do as the director of those banquets of friendship and poetry: Among all the voices of contemporary Spanish poetry, flame and death in Aleixandre, immense wing in Alberti, tender lily in Moreno Villa, Andean torrent in Pablo Neruda, intimate familial voice in Salinas, dark waters of the grotto in Guillén, tenderness and grief in Altolaguirre – to mention distinctly individual poets – Luis Cernuda's lofty voice has an original sound, its disturbing beauty unprotected by wire fences or moats.[19]

The lyrical effervescence of those years acquired a new dimension with Pablo Neruda's active political and poetic presence. This is documented in the existence of *Caballo verde para la poesía,* whose editorship was provided him by Spanish poets. But let us not be historically inaccurate. In a panoramic view of the artistic life of Madrid during that time, Neruda undoubtedly was not the supreme figure who dominated the literary scene. He was one among eight or ten – which was no small accomplishment at the moment when such extraordinary figures as Unamuno, Machado, Juan Ramón Jiménez, Valle Inclán, Azorín, García Lorca, Guillén, Aleixandre, Cernuda, etc., were stalking through the streets of Madrid. He was one among several, but one who at a certain moment succeeded in deposing Juan Ramón Jiménez from his pontifical chair of poetry and from his control of the gates to Parnassus. Neruda was the leader of a new movement in which almost all the important young poets enlisted, at times very fleetingly, with Miguel Hernández in the forefront. It is not my intention to claim for Pablo Neruda a position not rightfully his, but neither should he be denied, through neglect, the prominent place that at that historical moment he unquestionably was victorious in achieving.

Boston University

---

[19] Jorge Guillén, *Federico en persona,* pp. 30-31.

IV

THE AWAKENING TO A
NEW ESTHETIC

The Poetics of Social Awareness
in the Generation of 1936

PAUL ILIE

The existence of a Generation of 1936 cannot be doubted, but even if it were not a fact, the idea would have to be invented by liberal intellectuals. It is a concept that reflects the concerns of the left wing much more than the right, with the very date keeping alive the memory of the Civil War. As a rule, the victors of any struggle do not have to look back upon or relive the causes and ill effects of past violence. The vanquished, however, do precisely that, and in the case of the Spanish Republic, its sympathizers in every nation continue to discuss the issues surrounding the downfall of a democracy.

Consequently, when a definition of the Generation of 1936 is formulated, it emerges from the shadow of civil catastrophe. Not only is it often represented as a group whose members were prevented by war from fulfilling their literary promise, but its poetry has been seen to reflect the condition of a society recovering from deep internal wounds. Such negative factors are not likely to be emphasized by right-wing intellectuals, since the latter are absorbed with the "positive" features of a nation supposedly progressing towards normalcy. The liberals, on the other hand, are consistently critical of Spain's post-war situation, and they are quick to find literary evidence of discontent and generational malaise in a society whose destiny lies in what they consider to be dubious hands. Thus, it is in the interest of liberals that an unambiguous profile of the Generation of 1936 be delineated. Proof of this is the fact that the 1967 symposium at Syracuse University allowed the figure of Miguel Hernández to dominate the literary forums, whereas Dionisio Ridruejo received scant attention. It is also significant that the first important discussion of this Generation took place on foreign soil rather than at a Spanish academy, and that the Spaniards who participated were, in one way or another, estranged from their professional lives in Spain.

One problem, therefore, in dealing with the Generation of 1936 is to determine the degree to which the latter may be a liberal concept. A second problem, which results from the first, concerns the ambiguous nature of the poetry itself. A given theme can be open to opposing interpretations, depending upon whether the critic is liberal or conservative. To speak of *pan, pueblo,* and *libertad* is not necessarily to write protest literature, since these terms are as much a part of the fascist rhetoric as they are integral to leftist vocabulary. Moreover, poets living and publishing in Spain must submit either to a self-imposed or a governmental censorship, and this leads to a crucial linguistic ambiguity. Words can be used to evoke their opposite meaning, or the same words can be coined in counterfeit by state propagandists. For example, the declared value of a word might be "bread" or "freedom", but the real currency value would depend upon the speaker or listener. Liberal ears in Spain will hear "bread" and "freedom" and will think instead of "privation" and "repression", whereas to the right wing these words are the accurate slogans of their government's program. Such themes, therefore, can suggest either social protest or confirmation of a policy supposedly in effect, depending on which ideology is used to interpret them.

Beyond these difficulties, there is also the problem of which poets to include in the Generation of 1936. Clearly, the Civil War must be a factor in the development of their sensibility if the date 1936 is to have any significance. This means that members of the group had to be aware of what political issues were at stake at the outbreak of the war, and this in turn requires them to have been intellectually appreciative of the Republic as an alternative to dictatorship and monarchism in 1930–31. In other words, members of the Generation could not have been younger than 14 or 15 years in 1930–31, which is to say, they had to be born in 1916 at the latest. To include writers who were adolescents at the outbreak of the war in 1936 would be a mistake, because they could not have felt the war's true cultural impact at that age, that is, an intelligible imprint that went beyond emotional trauma. On the other hand, anyone born before 1905 would probably have participated in the vanguard movements of the 1920s, and consequently would have had a different intellectual formation.

On the basis of birth date and a manifest social awareness, therefore, the following poets will be discussed in this essay : Victoriano Crémer (1906), Gabriel Celaya (1911), Ildefonso Manuel Gil and Dionisio Ridruejo (1912), Ramón de Garciasol (1913), and Blas de Otero (1916). Also included will be Angela Figuera Aymerich (1903), since she is the only poetess of merit who can represent a woman's point of view. Other poets of this Generation who are of lesser interest from the standpoint of social poetics are Luis Felipe Vivanco (1907), Leopoldo Panero (1909), Luis Rosales (1910), José Luis Cano (1912) and Germán Bleiberg (1915). The poetry of Miguel Hernández (1910) has been omitted from this study because it is already so well known.[1]

[1]Wherever possible, references will be to complete works or to readily accessible anthologies. Quotations are from:
Antología de "Adonais", 2da ed. (Madrid, 1956).
José Maria Castellet, *Veinte años de poesía española* (Barcelona, 1960).
María de Gracia Ifach, *Cuatro poetas de hoy* (Madrid, 1960).
Leopoldo de Luis, *Poesía social* (Madrid, 1965).
Manuel Mantero, *Poesía española contemporánea* (Barcelona, 1966).
Antonio Molina, *Poesía cotidiana* (Madrid, 1966).
Gabriel Celaya, *Poesía (1934–61)* (Madrid, 1962).
Victoriano Crémer, *Caminos de mi sangre* (Madrid, 1947).
Ramón de Garciasol, *Defensa del hombre* (Madrid, 1950).
Ildefonso-Manuel Gil, *Poesía* (Zaragoza, 1953).
Blas de Otero, *Hacia la inmensa mayoría* (Buenos Aires, 1962).
　　　　　Esto no es un libro (Río Piedras, 1963).
Dionisio Ridruejo, *Hasta la fecha* (Madrid, 1961).
Luis Felipe Vivanco, *Continuación de la vida* (Madrid, 1949).
　　　　　Lecciones para el hijo (Madrid, 1961).

The starting point for any discussion of a socially-oriented poetry must be to determine whether the adoption of a social poetic was based on political commitment or literary principle. It is easy to say that the two are often inseparable, but it is also true that politically committed writers often keep their work free from social commentary, while, conversely, socially realistic themes can be treated for their esthetic value alone, without any particular ideological motivation behind them. In the case of the Generation of 1936, the poets are primarily writers who were aware of their literary antecedents, and it is their rejection of the *poesía pura* of the 1920s, rather than their political reaction to Spain's crisis, which regulates their attitude toward the forms and functions of poetry. Without doubt, the crisis precipitated their artistic response to society, but from the standpoint of poetics, the significant factor is the revaluation of language and themes. It is this new outlook which determined the nature of their work and, indeed, permitted the appearance of purely social concerns.

If, for example, these poets had elected to continue the lyrical and meta-physical trends set by Guillén and Salinas, or the surrealist moods invoked by Lorca and Aleixandre, then the sharp social tone of the Generation of 1936 would never have been manifested. This is precisely what happened in the cases of Bleiberg, Rosales, Panero and others, a fact which makes it difficult to justify their inclusion in the Generation except by accident of birth. At best, their social attitudes exist in symbolic form, concealed by literary escapism, lyrical fantasy, subjectivism or withdrawal. On the other hand, what happened to the social poets was just the opposite. The most famous examples are Hernández, who turned his back on surrealism after *Perito en lunas,* and Cela, who turned to neorealist prose after the surrealist *Pisando la dudosa luz del día.* More signifi-cant, however, is Crémer's transformation of the surrealist residue in *Caminos de mi sangre* for the sake of describing the chaotic national condition. The murky emotions and nightmarish landscapes of some members of the Generation of 1927, as well as the private intellectualism of other members, were viewed by the younger generation as evasions of social reality. One reason for this attitude was that experiments in cubism and *creacionismo,* for example, had reduced the degree of emotional involvement with human existence. As Gil wrote, "Busqué siempre en mis versos / un humano temblor, aunque sabía / que los mármoles tersos, / pura geometría, / resisten más el peso de los días" (*Poesía,* p. 60). ("In my verse I always strove for / a human tremor, although I knew / that terse marble, / pure geometry, / can withstand better the weight of the days.")

This abstract quality in experimental literature had removed the weight of reality and its problems from the poet's shoulders, providing him with a world of formal beauty to substitute for the disarray of the real world. However, this estheticist stance was inadmissible after 1936. It might have been defensible in 1927 on the grounds that artistic exclusivism was an international phenomenon in the aftermath of World War One, and perhaps it was even more justifiable in 1890, when the artist felt alienated from the bourgeois world. But, after the Civil War, the ugly and inhuman Spanish city eliminated escapism as an option for the intellectual elite, and the old class distinctions were liquidated as every citizen fell into one all-inclusive category of economic misery. For the artistic minority, as Figuera observed, "crear belleza pura, inútil, y cruel en su exclusividad, ya no es bastante. Hay que hacer algo más con la poesía, que es mi herramienta" (Luis, p. 66). ("It is not enough to create a beauty that is pure, useless, and cruel in its exclusiveness. Something more must be done with poetry, which is my work-tool.") Thus, the poet abandons his cult and becomes an ordinary citizen, declaring with Celaya, "Yo me alquilo por horas, río y lloro con todos; / pero escribiría un poema perfecto / si no fuera indecente hacerlo en estos tiempos" (Poesía, p. 201). ("I hire myself out for hours, I laugh and weep with everyone; / but I would write a perfect poem / if it were not indecent to do so in these times.")

Declarations of this type mark a fundamental break with the traditional concept of artistic privilege, a notion which artists have always treasured. Whether obliged to seek wealthy patrons, as in earlier centuries, or bent on extracting a rich bohemian life out of poverty, artists have always been aware of creating a vision that somehow transcended the value structure of the everyday world. Now, however, poets like Celaya may *wish* to write pretty poems, as others may wish to transcend reality by methods other than estheticism, but they must not, due to a moral sense that has been activated by social catastrophe. Instead, they say "maldigo la poesía concebida como un lujo / cultural por los neutrales / que, lavándose las manos, se desentienden y evaden. / Maldigo la poesía de quien no toma partido hasta mancharse" (Poesía, p. 366). ("I damn the poetry which is conceived of as a cultural luxury by neutral people who stand apart and evade things by washing their hands. / I damn the poetry of those who don't take a stand and get themselves dirty.") Such words need not be a call to specific political strategy. But they add up to a clear indictment of most modern poetry, the kind that keeps its moral superiority by refusing to dirty itself with partisan issues and which, consequently, loses its relevance by becoming a luxury item for the selfish few. Poetry no longer is "gota a gota pensada. / No es un bello producto. No es un fruto perfecto. / Es algo como el aire que todos respiramos" (Poesía, p. 366). ("Thought out bit by bit. / It is not a beautiful product. It is not a perfect fruit. It is something like the air we all breathe.") What is involved here is a new ethic of commitment and creative economy. Not only is ornamentalism attacked as an expensive commodity in the marketplace of 1936, but the leisurely attitude toward time is also criticised as a vestige of a now-lost prosperity, where neutral, speculative minds once devised concepts and metaphors that circulated on the curb exchange of the privileged elite.

This rejection of estheticism has its psychological counterpart in the new role of subjective feeling. Like intellectual exclusivism, emotional privacy is an untenable value because it caters to the individual's personal needs to the detriment of the group's. Moreover, subjectivism leads to a distortion of truth because it contemplates the world from a selfish perspective. Still worse, the preoccupation with the self is a useless narcissism that reflects paralysis, not analysis, and terminates in psychic dissolution, not in the resolution of the problem. In other words, the subjective stance lacks personal and social validity, and in fact it stands in the way of the collective good. This conflict can be seen in Gil's early poetry, where in one place he states, "Canto la pesadumbre / del doliente vivir que es mi destino", ("I sing the sorrow / of the painful life which is my destiny") while in another he admits, "Igual que un río desbordado rompe / la lineal dictadura de su cauce, / yo deseo evadirme de mí mismo" (*Poesía*, pp. 60, 81). ("Like an overflowing river that breaks / the dictatorial lines of its bed, / I wish to avoid my own self.")

The contradiction in Gil's sentiments betrays the real failure of subjectivism in Spanish poetry after 1936. Before the war, the subjective mode could be upheld as an alternative to a banal, insensitive world. Alternatively, it provided a method for adjusting to the disparity between social norms and personal idiosyncracies. But the premise in both cases was that something normal did exist in society, whatever the poet's evaluation of it might have been. Now, however, social reality is itself without norms, and the self has lost its standard of comparison. The poet's crisis is the crisis of society, and no manner of introspection will relieve the situation. This is again revealed in Gil's anguish, by means of a surrealist imagery which describes the man and his country in the same terms : "Hay una sequedad del alma, hay un regusto de muerte en nuestros labios, / ... y sabemos que es falsa la quietud de los muertos ... / La memoria del hombre se puebla de fantasmas". ("There is a dryness of soul, a faint taste of death on our lips, / ... and we know that the stillness of the dead is false ... / Man's memory is filled with ghosts.") His feelings, although private, are dominated by a collective despair, so that the poem is almost more descriptive of Spain as a nation, and in any case is symbolic of the Civil War trauma : "Mi poema recoge ese grito angustioso del terror milenario" (*Poesía*, pp. 57-58). ("My poem gathers that anguished cry of terror of the millenium.")

With a recognition of the futility of subjectivism, the poets react in two ways that acknowledge the greater importance of society over the individual as a literary theme. One reaction is the feeling of guilt, as when Celaya confesses : "Me avergüenza pensar cuánto he mimado / mis penas personales ... / Hoy quiero ser un canto ... / Cuando canta un poeta como cantan las hojas / ... No se expresa a sí mismo" (*Poesía*, pp. 291-292). ("I am ashamed to think of how much I coddled / my personal grief ... / Today I wish to be a song ... / When a poet sings as leaves do / ... he doesn't express himself.") The poet is shamed by his selfish preoccupations, and he points tacitly to the divorce between himself and the mass of humanity that shares most of his problems. Seeing beyond himself, he realizes that "mientras haya en el mundo tantos infortunados / buscar la salvación personal es mezquino" (*Cuatro poetas*, p. 96). ("While there are so many unfortunates in the world / it is petty to seek personal salvation.")

This leads to the second type of response affirming social, rather than private, values : the return to the collectivity. As Celaya proclaims, "Salgo del laberinto de mi yo. Canto el hecho / de unos hombres vulgares" (*Cuatro poetas*, p. 118). ("I emerge from the labyrinth of my self. I sing the fact of some ordinary men.") The emergence takes several forms, including another kind of isolation which is no longer introspective but remains no less individualistic. For example, Ridruejo explains how, in the manner of Fray Luis de León, "yo también querría / alejarme, del monte en la ladera, / ... Y luego regresar : El peso oscuro / de la cadena del esclavo, abajo / ... Querría. Pero vuelvo y es ahora / cuando estoy lleno de la tierra y tiemblo / como un pueblo que sufre" (*Hasta la fecha*, pp. 516-517). ("I too would like / to get away, on the mountainside, /

... And then to return : the heavy weight of the slave's chain, below / ... I would like to. But I return and it is now / that I am filled with the earth and tremble / like a suffering people.") Passages like this one develop a spiritual tone, but the presence of Nature, landscape, and simple folk prevent the cultivation of a semi-religious feeling of the kind expressed by Otero and Rosales. In Ridruejo and Celaya, an explicit identification with the people occurs that anchors the poetry to a genuine rural reality. The result is that subjectivism becomes irrelevant because the self finally has somewhere to go. The reference to the self as "un pueblo que sufre" ("a suffering people") is far removed from the notion of saving the artist's self from vulgarization. Indeed, the relationship between poet and people here is also different from the romantic admiration and longing which the former had for the latter. The Generation of 1936 postulates a common origin, a physical kinship rather than a spiritual one, rooted in land, common ancestry and shared social experiences.

The idea that the lifeline between the poet and the people runs through the land and a common heritage is most obviously characteristic of Hernández' poetry. But it is more subtly found in a poem by Garciasol that reveals the wisdom of seeking activity in an area which is healthier than the labyrinth of introspection : "Es tiempo de saber, de ver en hombre / la tremenda verdad de que es basura, / carne de cementerio . . . pero basura / que siente, que padece, que se hombrea / tal vez con Dios . . . / Quiero servir, ser útil" (*Defensa,* pp. 13, 18). ("It is time to learn, to see in man / the tremendous truth that he is garbage, / carrion for the cemetery . . . but garbage / that feels, suffers, acts like a man / with God perhaps . . . / I want to serve, to be useful.") Although Garciasol's evaluation of mankind is unflattering, he has used subjectivism as a method for abandoning his useless introspection. Moreover, he sees the dignity of the flesh as well as its baseness, and understands that sensitivity – once a subjective value – unites all men through the common bond of suffering. Thus, the poet is prepared to approach the collectivity in a useful manner.

There exists, then, a community of emotions that displaces private feeling and becomes one aspect of the sensibility of social awareness. In an afflicted society, each man is affected emotionally by the character of the larger affliction. Although private emotions will vary according to each individual, every man has a similar social plight, and in this area their psychological response will show little variation. What emerges, consequently, is a correspondence of feelings that brings all men together into an emotional unity that is lacking in the political realm. The merger of the intelligentsia and the masses, the affective identification of the one with the other, is reinforced by the fact that economic differences have been wiped out. It is the common link that is important, however, rather than the degree of suffering or penury, and, indeed, while most of the sentiments are pessimistic in tone, they are also hopeful in certain cases.

In this sense, therefore, we may speak of the political roots of pain. The emotional texture of the poems is coarsened by the harsh experiences of society. There is also, of course, a carryover of the sentimental gloom that had arisen during the Romantic period, a bleakness that had its origins in political disillusion. But there, the expression of anguish had always been personal, whereas in the Generation of 1936 both the roots of pain and the flower of its expression belong to the suffering of the collectivity. As Celaya indicates to Otero while they both confront the "irónicos zumbidos de aviones que pasan / y muertos boca arriba" (" ironic buzz of the passing airplanes / and the dead lying face up"), the destructive element in life has a long history, and "nuestra pena es tan vieja que quizá no sea humana / . . . Mas es el mundo entero quien se exalta en nosotros" (*Poesía,* pp. 218-219). ("Our grief is so old that it is perhaps not human / . . . But it is the whole world that is exalted in us.")

Given the community of feeling and the guilt over subjectivism, there is little doubt about what the poet's role should be. Since he is articulate, he can speak for the people even while feeling and suffering as they do. Ridruejo's invocation to his fellow poets is, "Vosotros, que volvéis del sobrecogimiento / para recomponer el mundo incomprensible" (*Hasta la fecha,* p. 474). ("You, who have recovered from your surprise / to recompose the incomprehensible world.") He sees the poet as having shaken off his personal anguish and recognizing the task ahead. Celaya goes even farther, and, like a laborer, tells Basterra that they are "pese a todo unidos como trabajadores. / Estábamos unidos por la común tarea, / por quehaceres viriles . . . / . . . poco sentimentales / . . . arreglar como sea esta máquina hoy mismo" (*Poesía,* p. 239). ("In spite of everything united like workers. / We were united by the common task, / by manly jobs . . . / . . . hardly sentimental / . . . to fix this machine today in any way.") There is no question about their energy, and as for their solidarity with the working man, its egalitarian vulgarity is well expressed by Otero : "Ando buscando un verso que supiese / parar a un hombre en medio de la calle, / un verso en pie – ahí está el detalle – / que hasta diese la mano y escupiese" (*Cuatro poetas,* p. 156). ("I go searching for a verse that can / stop a man in the middle of the street, / a verse on its feet – that's the point – /that can even shake hands and spit.")

Popular alignment and dedication do not mean, however, that every poet in the Generation is equally confident of fulfilling his task. The doubts raised by Garciasol contain a serious question : "Dentro de mí no estoy en paz madura, / . . ni mis manos / pueden traer el pan que nos libere / . . . habrá un día / sin odio justo y santa violencia, / cerca en el tiempo, para mí imposible" (*Defensa,* p. 41). ("Within myself there is no full-grown peace, / . . . nor can my hands / bring the bread that will free us / . . . there will be a day / without holy violence or just hatred, /near in time, impossible for me.") That is, has the Generation of 1936 achieved a sufficient degree of inner peace to write the kind of poetry that will free citizens from their hatred and pent-up violence? Garciasol, evidently, has not, for his own introspection has shown him that recent memories of civil tragedy prevent him from kneading the bread of freedom, which requires hands steadied by hope and tranquility. Thus, Garciasol's feeling of solidarity with the worker may be just as strong as Otero's, but he must nevertheless admit, "No tengo que dar nada, que soy nada / . . . Puedo daros / . . . palabras, no cuchillos para el nudo / hecho de hambres y miedos que os amarga" (*Defensa,* pp. 21-23). ("I don't have to give anything, for I am nothing / . . . I can give you / . . . words, not knives for the knot / made of hunger and fear that embitters you.") On the other hand, despite this inadequacy, the poet's self-image is unambiguous. He distinguishes three types of men : good, ordinary people, the victimizers of the latter, and artists who feel "la diferencia / que me hace clandestino y peligroso / para el hijo del mal, que quiere al hombre, / señor de libertad y amor, esclavo" (*Defensa,* p. 22). ("The difference / that makes me secretive and dangerous / to the son of evil, who wishes to enslave man, / the lord of liberty and love.") The poet's identification with the masses makes him dangerous, and yet the reason is not the power of poetry but the strength of the masses themselves. Clearly, Garciasol has just confessed that he is incapable of composing emancipatory verse. However, his very support of the people is enough to make him feared by the oppressor as a hidden source of popular inspiration. The masses are strong enough; what they need is a stimulant within their own ranks to activate that strength.

This idea of the poet as an agent or source of intelligence is developed by Crémer, who sees his mission as the enlightenment of the unthinking man : "yo quiero llegarle con mi verso; / romper el duro mármol de su frente; / darme en pan de sus hambres; ser su llanto. . . ." (*Caminos,* p. 51). ("I want to reach him with my verse; / crack the hard marble of his forehead; / give myself as bread for his hunger; be his lament. . . .") Such a role makes Crémer as much of a threat as Garciasol suggested, and in fact he states elsewhere that the concept of "social poetry" is feared because the term contains extra-literary overtones : "Por el camino de 'lo social' – se piensa maliciosamente – lo mismo en poesía que en política o en economía, se llega a 'lo revolucionario', y la sola enunciación de la palabra pone temblores en muchos ánimos más bien de vuelo corto" (Luis, pp. 85-86). ("It is maliciously thought that the road of "social" awareness – in poetry as well as in politics or economics – is the way to "revolution", and the mere mention of the word sends shudders into many people of rather limited vision.") Thus, Crémer is realistic enough to know that inspiring the masses is not enough, and that political power is also needed to improve their plight. This, then, implies a pre-revolutionary stage in the role of poetry, the poetics of which includes an attitude of articulate confidence in the value of writing verse. For even when the poet feels ineffective, his poem can be a modest reflection of the situation. As Gil expresses this limitation, "Yo quiero escribir un poema / sin palabras, / en el que se cantan las cosas sencillas, / las vidas calladas" (*Poesia,* p. 14). ("I want to write a poem / without words, / where simple things / and silent lives are sung.")

The real issue, then, is the need for articulateness. The feeling of solidarity eliminates the old categories of "intellectual" and "worker", and introduces a distinction based on means or skills rather than rank or job. In this case, the skill is eloquence, not manual dexterity. Thus, all poets are workers, just as all carpenters are workers, but not all workers can be either poets or carpenters, and no one group can match what another group excels at. Each man does what he is best able to do, and what poets can do best is to bring words into the oppressive silence that fills men's lives. At worst, he can give voice to the people's unspoken pain by describing their wretched condition, and at best, he can speak out against the causes of their oppression, thus shattering another kind of silence : that maintained by the official establishment. In the poetics of social awareness, the writer's duty is to raise his voice in whatever manner the political situation will allow. This, of course, varies with the times. In 1955, for example, Otero could say, "Escribo / en defensa del reino / del hombre y su justicia.

Pido / la paz / y la palabra" ("I write / in defense of the kingdom / of man and his justice. I ask for / peace / and the chance to speak"), whereas in 1960 he wrote in Mexico, "Escribo / por necesidad, / para / contribuir / (un poco) / a borrar / la sangre / y / la iniquidad / del mundo / (incluida la caricaturesca españa actual)" (*Inmensa mayoría,* pp. 110, 122). ("I write / out of necessity, / in order to / contribute / (a little) / to wiping away / the blood / and / the iniquity / of the world / (including today's caricaturesque spain.") But whatever the date, the underlying principle is that "la poesía tiene sus deberes. / ... Entre ella y yo hay un contrato / social" (Luis, p. 147). ("Poetry has its duties. / ... Between it and me is a social / contract.")

The imperative of articulation includes not only description but protest. It is the ability to say "no" to the agents of a regime bent on carrying out the injustices of a minority will. A good example of this comes, appropriately enough, from the lips of a woman, as Angela Figuera exclaims, "no quiero / que en los labios se encierren mentiras, / ... que en la cárcel se encierre a los buenos. / ... No quiero / que mi hijo desfile ... / No quiero / que me tapen la boca / cuando digo NO QUIERO" (Luis, pp. 81-82). ("I don't want / lips to bear lies, / ... good people to be locked in jail. / ... I don't want / my son to march. ... / I don't want / my mouth to be muzzled / when I say I DON'T WANT.") Such words represent a deliberately heroic attempt to challenge the will of authority. The poet must be ready to specify the wrongs which he is accusing the regime of perpetrating, and he must be prepared to expose himself to the risk, perhaps the certainty, of reprisal. Figuera is well aware of the danger, and to avoid all equivocation she bluntly urges the poet to approach whenever he sees a prison or pointed guns, and "a pecho descubierto, / lanza un tremendo NO que salve el mundo" (Luis, p. 80). ("With breast uncovered, / launch a tremendous NO that will save the world.")

The poet's heroism is not, however, a reckless and romantic position. It is considered, weighed, and formed in a quasi-existentialist framework. The truth is, in Celaya's words, "Da miedo ser poeta. ... / Da miedo decir alto lo que el mundo silencia. / ... soy responsable / de todo lo que siento y en mi se hace palabra" (*Poesía,* p. 266). ("It is frightening to be a poet. ... / It is frightening to say aloud what is silenced by the world. / ... I am responsible / for everything I feel and is verbalized in me.") A choice is involved – to face fear or avoid it – and an ethical context must be evaluated – the social conditions that promulgate fear. Hence, the concept of duty implies a response to poetic reality as well as to political situations. The poet is obligated to report not only what can be seen by every member of the body politic, but also what cannot be seen, namely, his private feelings about the situation. This involves a double duty, for he is morally bound both to his private emotional world, a realm which artists normally protect from society, and to the social environment which has trapped him. Once the poet recognizes these obligations, it becomes virtually impossible for him to remain obedient to an unjust state. He must speak out, as Garciasol does : "No me puedo callar ya más. No vale / para imponer silencio el latigazo / que me cruza la boca" (Luis, p. 131). ("I can no longer remain silent. Worthless now / is the whiplash across my face / to impose silence.") In one sense, perhaps, he really has no choice, because "si me callo, me condeno; / si no me callo, me callan, / que algún maleficio enreda / y trastrueca mis palabras" (*Defensa*, p. 38). ("If I remain silent, I condemn myself; / if I don't remain silent, they silence me, / for a certain spell encircles / and twists my words.") Hence the poet's reaction in writing, done in such a way as to expose himself to a minimum of risks while depicting the social reality that he wishes to describe.

His method in that depiction has become one of the central strategies of Spanish neorealism. It consists of presenting life as it is, without making value judgments. This technique has been especially suitable to the novel, as in the case of *La colmena,* where conditions condemn themselves merely by being shown, without moral commentaries on the part of the author. In poetry, however, the case is somewhat different, because even though certain adversities are described, they are less significant than the fundamental tone of social awareness in the poems. That is, poets talk about the *problem* of writing social literature, or the need to do so. In this way, they avoid direct criticism of society while alluding to its troubled situation by references to their own role as socially-oriented poets. For example, instead of writing about abject working conditions, unemployment or the lack of political representation, poets like Ridruejo, Celaya, Otero and Garciasol develop a cult of "the people" in their verse. This mystique reflects the poet's awareness of being a potential leader, which is where the social criticism enters. As the new spokesman for the people, the poet allows his nominal role to call attention to the failure of politics. The poet's replacement of the politician as the leader of the masses implies that the latter's interests have not been properly looked after.

Let us note how this cult of the *pueblo* differs from the romantic tradition, where the values of simplicity, robustness and proximity to Nature had characterized the image of the common man. In the Generation of 1936, there is no exaltation of a romantic folk-concept. Instead, the humble and sometimes destitute existence of the masses becomes symbolic of the poet's own impotence. Similarly, the untapped strength of the peasant is often mentioned, and this is a reminder of the poet's own urge to rise up and act. Thus, the poetry of this Generation suggests not only political failure but the failure of intellect in general. There are no political ideas, no allusions to new or alternative governments, no affirmation of art or intellectual values. The only culture-saving factor is the *pueblo,* whose reservoir of vitality must be drawn upon in order to assure the future well-being of the nation. However, by extolling this group value, the poet admits that his own salvation depends upon the people, and not upon creative impulse. Indeed, the social poet has no other theme, and his destiny is nourished by the soil instead of by his ideas and metaphors.

The image of the *pueblo* presented by the Generation of 1936 is fairly standard, with nothing new or dramatic to distinguish it from the one conceived by the Generation of 1898. Its features are somewhat harsher, and the picture is perhaps more poignant, as in Garciasol's poem, where "hay miradas, silencios minerales / de acusación en estas pobres gentes / armadas de razón hasta los dientes" (Luis, p. 137). ("There are glances, mineral silences / filled with accusation among these poor people / armed to the teeth with reason.") But even here, one senses a trace of guilt on the part of the poet, as if he were imagining an accusation on the peasants' faces, a fantasy that originates in his feelings of guilt and inadequacy over not helping them in their need. The fact is that the poet's faith in the common man is hard to justify in terms of how he is actually represented. When Celaya fondly proclaims "Sancho-vulgo, Sancho-ibero, / porque tú existes, existen aún mi patria y mi esperanza" (*Poesía*, p. 342), ("Sancho-everyman, Iberian Sancho, / because you exist, my country and my hope still exist"), it is really an abstraction that he is cherishing, not a realistic presence.

What is left, therefore, is a situation that thrusts the poet back upon himself. The masses depend upon him for the missing political leadership, even though he cannot lead because of the censors. And he depends upon the masses for his hope in the future, even though they have no way of throwing off their shackles. Given this impasse, the poet retreats to a familiar fortress : his own concept of what poetry should be doing. This is best formulated by Celaya, whose experience with the problem of collective impotence is expressed in practical, economic terms : "Nosotros no tenemos problemas trascendentales; / tenemos hambre y frío . . . / . . . el alma es un lujo para privilegiados / . . . Quienes mueren por falta de pan o unas monedas / . . . no explican qué les pasa, ni piensan. . . ." (*Cuatro poetas,* p. 96). ("We don't have transcendental problems; / we are hungry and cold . . . / . . . souls are a luxury for the privileged / . . . Those who die for want of bread or cash / . . . don't think or explain what is happening to them. . . .") And so, by extension, since the poet has linked his destiny to the people's, the role of poetry must be immediate and practical. As Figuera urges, "Hay que hacer algo más con la poesía, que es mi herramienta. . . . Desenterremos sus bellezas esenciales : el trabajo, el amor, la unión, el valor de lo humilde. . . ." (Luis, p. 66). ("Something more must be done with poetry, which is my work-tool. . . . Let us disinter its essential beauties : work, love, union, the value of what is humble.") Poetry is steel, says Garciasol, and the poet is the man who alloys it : "verso de carne de trabajadores . . . yo trabajador soy y me llamo" (Luis, p. 137). ("The verse of workingmen's flesh . . . I am and call myself a workingman.") More specifically, in Celaya's words, the poet is "un ingeniero del verso y un obrero / que trabaja con otros a España en sus aceros" (*Cuatro poetas,* p. 116). ("An engineer of verse and worker / who with others forges Spain in their steelworks.") These images imply more than a merely partisan expression of unity with the working class. They indicate a confidence in the feasibility of poetry to perform socially useful tasks. For Celaya, "la poesía es un arma cargada de futuro" ("poetry is a weapon loaded with the future"), a basic item in the list of daily staples : "poesía para el pobre, poesía necesaria / como el pan de cada día" (*Poesía*, p. 365). ("Poetry for the poor, poetry as necessary / as daily bread.")

Thus, poetry is asserted to have an indispensable utilitarian role. But this affirmation is really an act of transcending the sphere of material need. It converts the poetic word into a source of spiritual comfort, thereby contradicting the stated practical goal. Of course, to the extent that spiritual nourishment can be as useful as actual food, Celaya's poems may be regarded as serving a utilitarian purpose. But in a hungry society there is no substitute for food, and so when the poet exclaims "demos de comer al hambriento" ("let us give the hungry food"), but means by this "cantemos para todos los que, aún humillados, aun martirizados, sienten la elevadora y combativa confianza propia de los . . . vivos" (Luis, p. 105), ("let us sing for all those who, still humbled, still martyrized, feel the elevating and combative confidence that belongs to . . . the living"), we are forced to conclude that this is simply a well-intentioned piece of rhetoric. In such cases, social poetry in the Generation of 1936 becomes what the Spanish form of Catholicism has often been accused of : a socially useless palliative. This can be said without criticism, for the limits of poetry have always been painfully clear, just as the limits of Christianity have been exposed by Unamuno in *La agonía del cristianismo.*

The realization of this drawback causes a poet like Otero to despair of ever being effective, "porque escribir es viento fugitivo, / y publicar, columna arrinconada. / . . . torno a mi obra / más inmortal : aquella fiesta brava / del vivir y el morir" (*Inmensa mayoría,* p. 87). ("Because writing is like a fleeing wind, / and publishing, a corner column. / . . . I turn to my / more immortal work : that great fiesta / of living and dying.") For him, the moment of poetry's triumph has not yet arrived, although he hopes that "definitivamente, cantaré para el hombre./ Algún día – *después* – alguna noche,/ me oirán" (*Inmensa mayoría,* p. 35). ("Definitively, I will sing for man./ Some-day – *afterwards* – , some night, / they will hear me.") For this reason, the poet-workers of the Generation of 1936 base their social poetics on an unconscious transcendental principle. The poem is not so much a tool of society as it is a balm for the soul, and its medium of operation is the world of intangibles : emotion, idea, hope, regeneration. Thus, Gil's assurance that "sobre un mundo de ruinas y dolores/ se hará otra vez el verbo Poesía" (*Poesía,* p. 48), ("upon a world of ruins and sorrows / the word Poetry will again be made"), is really an article of faith. The engineer must believe in the idea of efficacy before he puts his machine into operation.

Indeed, as one reviews the work of these poets, the theme of hope gains prominence in precisely those areas where political action would be most effective. The metaphor of poetry as bread is a conspicuous example, but so too are the scenes of social disintegration in the poetry of Otero. His description of the impoverished miner, or of the dead city Madrid (Luis, pp. 146, 147), suggest conditions in which hope is the only recourse left to the Spanish people. Food, justice, beauty and truth are so alien to society that when Crémer alludes to "el clamor oscuro de los que tienen hambre" ("the dark clamor of those who are hungry"), he leaves very little else for them to hold on to : "la Verdad es una vieja coima, aletargada/ como un oscuro sapo al sol. Que la Justicia es una dueña zurcidora,/ y la Hermosura un inefable don, lejos del hombre" (*Caminos,* pp. 86-87). ("Truth is an old bawd, as lethargic / as a dark toad in the sun. Justice is a devious biddy, and Beauty an ineffable gift, distant from man.") What is left, then, is hope in the idea of a *pueblo,* of a Sancho Panza, of an endurable, unchanging entity which is no longer as mystical as the romantic concept, but which transcends history and will survive the adversities of the historical moment.

Hope also grows in another area touched upon by these poets : the future of the younger generation. "La juventud de hoy, la de mañana/ forja otro cielo rojo, audaz, sonoro" ("Today's youth, tomorrow's, / forges another red sky, audacious, loud"), asserts Otero (*Esto no es un libro*, p. 140), expressing faith in the capabilities of an age group he no longer belongs to. But by lauding the young people who are his juniors, he calls attention to the radical ineffectuality of his own generation. Thus, we can learn much about the real values of poets like Otero simply by examining their image of Spanish youth. As it turns out, they not only underscore their own failures and inadequacies by the method of contrasting example, but they cancel these failures by imagining an opposite set of virtues in the young. In other words, what the members of the 1936 group lack, they think they find dormant in the character and potential works of the generation that will follow. However, this kind of hope is little more than wishful thinking, the desire to see the promise of youth fulfilled, the need to believe that one's own sins will be expiated.

Thus, while Figuera declares "cuando observo/el puro resplandor de vuestras manos" ("when I observe/ the pure radiance of your hands"), she admits tacitly that the old guard has unclean hands; while she promises "no, no os diré del odio y la venganza" ("no, I won't speak to you of hatred and vengeance"), she implies that these are the emotions that have poisoned the minds of those old enough to remember. And so, with nothing more than hope, she proclaims to the young that "es vuestra hora./ ... Uníos ... Arrinconad banderas desteñidas,/ los libros de la Historia apolillados./ ... Labrad, edificad, haced España./ España en paz" (Castellet, pp. 369-371). ("It is your hour./ ... Unite ... Cast aside faded flags, / moth-eaten history-books. / ... Till, build, make Spain. / A Spain in peace.") All of her advice is based on the dismissal of the very social values which her own age had upheld and then had to live without : the banner of political parties, the awareness of history, peace. Moreover, the advice is virtually indistinguishable from the propaganda line of the right wing, and one wonders how such progressively-minded poets would have sounded had they not been so constantly exposed to the post-war Spanish environment. Here, then, is the crucial question. If the Generation of 1936 failed without the above-mentioned values, will the new guard be any more successful without them? What makes the older generation think that the young can do without those values? Its belief is based not so much on conviction as on faith, and on the need to find a redeeming surrogate for a generation stripped of its power to act. As a result, we discover a rhetoric of hope that may be positive in its outlook but which is empty in terms of recommending a social program for the nation's youth.

There are, to be sure, general affirmations, like Celaya's poem : "Los jóvenes obreros,/ los hombres materiales,/ la gloria colectiva del mundo del trabajo/ resuenan ..." (*Poesía*, p. 246). "Young workers,/ real, live men,/ the collective glory of the working world / resound ...") Or else there are niceties like Vivanco's innocuous *Lecciones para el hijo,* which seek to impart pedestrian feelings about God and life's obstacles, without any meaningful relation to society. But of all the poets, only Ridruejo seems to understand that his generation cannot expect to save the young from error, and that each generation must make its own mistakes, free of the crippling reliance which the old can impose on the young in their desire to be saved from their own helplessness. In Ridruejo's words, "¡Oh! no enseñes al joven;/no le digas mostrando tu pequeña impotencia :/

'Mirad, jóvenes, ésta, la verdad de la vida.'/ Que no sepan por ti . . . Pero no sabrán nada;/ sus ojos no te ven, sus oídos no escuchan/ . . . Ellos sabrán por sí y a costa de su sangre" (*Hasta la fecha*, p. 461). ("Oh, don't teach young people;/ don't say to them while showing your petty impotence :/ 'Look, youth, at this, life's truth !' / Let them not learn from you . . . But they won't know anything;/ their eyes do not see you, their ears do not listen / . . . They will learn by themselves and at the cost of their own blood.") This attitude is totally negative from the standpoint of social progress, but it represents an honest appraisal of the cultural gap that separates the generations. Furthermore, it affords a profound insight into the lack of political continuity in Spain, due to the inability of different age groups to communicate with each other after such dissimilar social experiences.

This inability to communicate is one explanation for the rise of religious poetry after the Civil War. Poets like Rosales, Vivanco and Bleiberg take the spiritual route to well-being because the political road is closed indefinitely. Rather than regarding poetry as the unifying vehicle of diverse social groups or of different ages, they see it as a private act of expression : of the self, of one's ideals, of God. Poetry is not used to communicate a program or social ideal to the public because this sphere of activity appears to be futile. Since it is impossible to take effective action under a dictatorship, the poet's alternatives are either silence or the expression of an inner experience. He chooses the latter and the result is largely a religious verse whose quest for salvation includes many possibilities, but not that of social materialism. The point is that this may not be a positive act of spiritual preference but a choice made out of default. Poets may not wish to reject the material world, but their religious poetry does precisely this because they are concerned about saving their consciousness, which can be done either by a literature of social protest or of transcendence.

The choice facing the poet is expressed very well by Vivanco in an "Elegía a Cervantes", where a disciple asks the master: "¿Debo flotar, con alma lejana, en la penumbra/ de esta iglesia . . . / o seguir con mi sombra solitaria hasta el campo,/ donde hace una mañana de brisa . . .?" ("Should I float, with distant soul, in the shade / of this church . . . / or continue with my solitary shadow to the fields,/ where the morning breeze rises . . .?") The answer is supplied by Vivanco's own career as a religious poet. Ironically, the poem appears in a collection whose title is *Continuación de la vida,* and indicates that at least in 1949 there were poets who could only conceive of carrying on in life under the auspices of religious experience. Consequently, we find poets like Rosales who write compositions with titles like "El Dios vivo" ("The Living God"), or "El desvivir del corazón" ("The Zealous Heart"). And in one case, there is the title "Va el Duero alabando a Dios" ("The river Duero goes praising God"), apropos of which it is presumably unfair to ask what the river Ebro was doing in the meantime.

On the other hand, some poets perceive the unconscious escapism that lay behind religious poetry. For example, Otero is interesting precisely because of a counterpoint of spiritual and social themes. His collection *Angel fieramente humano* is indeed introspective, religious and anguished, but his torment is presented symbolically, and it relates to the plight of those who came of age during the catastrophe: "Un mundo como un árbol desgajado./ Una generación desarraigada." ("A world like a tree torn up./ A generation uprooted.") Then in later years, the religious theme is transformed into protest: "Ciudad llena de iglesias/ y casas públicas . . ./ Laboriosa ciudad . . ./ donde el hombre maldice, mientras rezan/ los presidentes del consejo . . ." (*Inmensa mayoría, pp.* 11, 135). ("A city full of churches / and public buildings . . . / A laboring city . . . / where men curse / while council presidents pray . . .") This implies no lack of reverence, but rather, that a decision favoring social poetry has been made on the grounds that if devotional feeling still exists, God needs it less than the *pueblo,* and the poet does better by channeling his dedication toward the forsaken masses. As Figuera expresses it, "Señor, si no te canto no te enojes./Ya ves, no tengo tiempo para nada./. . . No te hago falta, tienes a tus Santos;/. . . Pero ¿quién baja un rayo/ de sol hasta las cárceles sin puerta?" (Luis, p. 78). ("Lord if I don't sing to you, don't be angry./ As you see, I have no time for anything. / . . . You don't need me, you have your Saints;/ . . . But who sends down a ray / of sunshine to the doorless prisons?") This apologizes for the lack of concern with spiritual problems in social poetry, but it is a justification that is unnecessary from the standpoint of poetic principles. Religious themes can indeed be introduced in support of social realism if the poet wishes, as in one of Crémer's poems, where God becomes a suffering peasant: "Dios de España / oloroso a herramienta, a sangre, a barro;/ un Dios pobre y cansado, nos abría / con dulzura los brazos . . . Dios estaba en nosotros, como el viejo/de la buhardilla, silencioso, inmenso . . ." (*Furia,* p. 12). ("God of Spain / smelling of tools, of blood, of clay;/ a poor and weary God, opened / his arms gently to us . . . God was within us, like the old man / in the garret, silent, immense . . . .")

This modification of a religious motif for a realist context illustrates the final principle in the social poetics of Crémer's generation. Secularization means neither a rejection of the Divine nor the abandonment of transcendental ideals. Instead, it indicates the establishment of priorities for a society which needs that first piece of bread before it can affirm "not by bread alone . . ." By implication, this idea also reveals a commitment to the collectivity at the expense of individual salvation. In the light of a culture whose history has often sacrificed worldly interests for the sake of spirit, this dedication marks the beginning of an emancipation from escapism. At the same time, it classifies poetry as a social phenomenon whose private sector consists of the poet's gesture of commitment to collective priorities. Thus, secularization on the one hand, and objectivization on the other provide, at least theoretically, a workable social poetic that can frame a general message for the group. The rest is a matter of particular programs or themes, which vary according to the times and the whims of the censors. Clearly the Generation of 1936 has set up the machinery. How well this machinery produces is relative to the standards of production which each critic is accustomed to seeing.

The University of Michigan

Blas de Otero:
The Past and the Present of "The Eternal"

EDMUND L. KING

Poesía social (social poetry). *Poesía realista* (realist poetry). The terms are interchangeable. They are even combinable in the well-known designation 'socialist realism'. Although Pedro Salinas used the term *poesía social* in his book on Rubén Darío in 1948, for our practical purposes, the presence of such poetry on the scene in Spain was discovered and extolled by José María Castellet in his anthology *Veinte años de poesía española, 1939–1959* (Twenty Years of Spanish Poetry, 1939–1959), first published in 1960. The polemic that ensued from Castellet's pronouncements need not concern us here. There is no doubt that something vaguely identifiable as *poesía realista* – the label preferred by Castellet – exists in post-war Spain, whether it is the only kind of poetry that ought to exist or not, and Castellet's characterization of it, though logically destructible, withstands the test of intuition.

That characterization is relevant to the question of the past and the present of "Lo eterno" (The Eternal), the prefatory poem in Blas de Otero's first volume of verse, *Angel fieramente humano* (Fiercely Human Angel – Madrid : Insula, 1950), and in view of this relevance I take the liberty of recalling Castellet's main points concerning what he calls "Tradición simbolista y actitud realista" (The symbolist tradition and the realist attitude) :[1]

1. Opposed to the poet of the symbolist tradition, who rejects the bourgeois society which has no place for him, the realist poet has a role in history which he may deny only under peril of betraying his conception of poetry and his social responsibility.

2. Opposed to the symbolist, who sees himself as a being apart with magical word power, the realist is a man among men, whose life in history is his subject.

3. Opposed to the mythico-symbolic abstraction of symbolist poetry, realist poetry will be historico-narrative.

4. Opposed to the esoteric, enigmatic language of symbolist musicality and sensual suggestion, the poetry of the realists will strive for a clear human meaning, expressed in plain colloquial language accessible to all men.

When Castellet speaks of symbolism, he means *modernismo* (modernism), the

[1]José María Castellet, *Veinte años de poesía española, 1939-1959* (2nd ed., Barcelona : Seix Barral, 1960), pp. 33-36.

125

synthesis of nineteenth-century Parnassianism, *symbolisme* and sensualism which was achieved not only but primarily by Rubén Darío for poetry throughout the Hispanic world, a combination of apparently incompatible elements that has proved remarkably stable, even though our taste is now cloyed by the early dishes cooked up with the ingredients. Broadly speaking, it is surely true that, with the possible exception of Unamuno, poetry in Spanish was for fifty years synonymous with *modernismo,* so that young poets in revolt against the premises of *modernismo* were bound to feel that they were almost in revolt against poetry itself. This love-hate relationship is particularly interesting in connection with "Lo eterno".

Before going into this relationship, we must clarify a detail of the bibliographical history of *Angel fieramente humano.* In the first edition we find on page 7, immediately after the copyright page, only the phrase "A la inmensa mayoría" (To the immense majority). Later, when the same work is republished as part of Otero's collected works by Losada (Buenos Aires, 1962), the phrase slightly altered is made the title for the entire volume, *Hacia la inmensa mayoría* (Toward the Immense Majority), and the section subtitled *Angel fieramente humano* is now introduced (p. 9) with a quotation from Rubén Darío: "Yo no soy un poeta *de mayorías;* pero sé que, indefectiblemente, tengo que ir a ellas." ("I am not a poet *of majorities;* but I know that I must, without fail, go to meet them.")

When we think that the post-war poets in Spain were repelled by the comfortable aestheticism of their immediately preceding generation, that they preferred, like most of us today, the human model of Antonio Machado to that of Juan Ramón Jiménez, we necessarily feel some surprise when Blas de Otero takes as his epigraph Rubén Darío's remark, even though it appears to serve his purposes. It is of course no secret that Rubén was more than a mere *modernista,* that *modernismo* was a garment he tried to put off once he had worn it out; and the famous remark, wrenched from its context, suggests the Rubén that a social poet might like to have as his prefiguration. However, the context in the preface to the *Cantos de vida y esperanza* (Songs of Life and Hope) tells us at once that Rubén had other things in mind:[2]

> ¿No es verdaderamente singular que en esta tierra de Quevedos y Góngoras los únicos innovadores del instrumento lírico, los únicos libertadores del ritmo, hayan sido los poetas del *Madrid Cómico* y los libretistas del género chico?
>
> Hago esta advertencia porque la forma es lo que primeramente toca a las muchedumbres.

....

[2] Rubén Darío, *Obras poéticas completas* (Madrid: Aguilar, 1967), pp. 625-626. "Is it not truly extraordinary that in this land of Quevedos and Góngoras the only innovators with the lyrical instrument, the only ones to free our rhythms, have been the poets of *Madrid Cómico* [a humor magazine] and the librettists of our musical comedies? I make this observation because what gets through to the masses first of all is form. . . . When I said that my poetry was mine, part of my being, I stated the first premise of my existence, without the slightest intention of causing others to take sides in either thought or purpose; and I spoke out of my intense love for beauty as an absolute."

Cuando dije que mi poesía era "mía, en mí" sostuve la primera condición de mi existir, sin pretensión ninguna de causar sectarismo en mente o voluntad ajena, y en un intenso amor a lo absoluto de la belleza.

Now we must ask why, in the sixteen words Blas de Otero lifts from this context to use as his epigraph – I have omitted them here on purpose – he underscores the phrase *de mayorías* (of majorities) : "Yo no soy poeta *de mayorías*" – he has Rubén say – "pero sé que, indefectiblemente, tengo que ir a ellas." There are no doubt various reasons for this trifling with typography. One evidently is that "*de mayorías*" is not what Rubén wrote. Blas de Otero here takes after his acknowledged master in literary cannibalism, Unamuno. What Rubén actually says is : "Yo no soy un poeta para las muchedumbres" (I am not a poet for the multitudes) – that is, he is not writing for either the readers of *Madrid Cómico* or for the audience of the *género chico* – "pero sé que indefectiblemente tengo que ir a ellas." The misquotation was obviously intentional, a gambit in poetic gamesmanship, and the game is to put Juan Ramón Jiménez in his place. For Juan Ramón, we may recall, had dedicated the *Segunda antolojía poética* (Madrid : Colección Universal, 1920) "a la minoría, siempre" (to the minority, always), and to this dedication, simple and clear enough, he adds, with his characteristic, exquisite narcissism, a few explanatory notes :

No creo . . . en un arte popular esquisito – sencillo y espontáneo – . Lo esquisito que se llama popular es siempre, a mi juicio, imitación o tradición inconsciente de un arte refinado que se ha perdido. Si el trianero inculto que pinta los cacharros, o la mujer lagarterana que borda las telas, se ponen a inventar, estropean el exorno. Lo hacen bien, porque copian inconscientemente un modelo escojido. La sencillez estética es un producto último . . . de cultura refinada (p. 322) . . . No creo . . . en un arte para la mayoría. Ni importa que la minoría entienda del todo el arte ; basta con que se llene de su honda emanación (p. 324).[3]

What Juan Ramón writes in 1920 is a variation on Rubén's theme, a positive statement – "a la minoría" – in place of "Yo no soy un poeta para las muchedumbres". Imitating Jiménez twice in one stroke, first by using a reversal of the phrase "a la minoría", second by half-quoting Darío, Blas de Otero turns Rubén's statement "tengo que ir a [las muchedumbres]" into the title of his collected poems, *Hacia la inmensa mayoría*. "Hacia las inmensas muchedumbres" (Toward the Immense Multitudes) would do, in an uneuphonious way, to invoke the patronage of Rubén Darío, but by substituting Juan Ramón's variation for Rubén's theme, Otero can enlist the patriarch of *modernismo* against the latter-

---

[3] "I do not believe that popular art can be exquisite – simple and spontaneous. When something exquisite is labeled folk-art it is always, in my opinion, the imitation or unconscious transmission of a refined art that has been lost. If the uncultured pottery-painter of Triana, or the embroideress from Lagartera, set to inventing, they spoil the design. They do their work well because they unconsciously copy a chosen model. Aesthetic simplicity is an end-product of refined culture. . . . I do not believe . . . in an art for the majority. Nor does it matter whether the minority understands art entirely; it suffices for the minority to be filled with art's deep emanation."

day archpriest of the movement, as if to say, Rubén has turned on his own followers. That Darío meant to say, in the preface to *Cantos de vida y esperanza,* no such thing as the isolated quotation imputes to him is not the point here. (If the scriptor were not allowed to quote the devil to his purpose, poetry would have no history.) The point is that one goes into the first poem in the book with the image of Rubén Darío in the front of one's mind, so that if the title "Lo eterno" does not recall a poem of Rubén's, the title plus the first line surely will, and if these together do not suffice, the encounter with other images and with certain metrical peculiarities will finally cause the reader to say to himself, "This reminds me of 'Lo fatal' ", again from the *Cantos de vida y esperanza.*

Emilio Alarcos Llorach, in the chapter entitled "Alusiones y préstamos literarios" of his helpful little book on Blas de Otero, groups the borrowings from other writers with Otero's similar borrowing of ready-made phrases from everyday language. These latter, he says, "Son a primera vista clisés, muletillas . . . Usa de ellas repristinándolas, esto es, analizándolas, haciendo revivir el sentido de sus elementos y produciendo así un efecto expresivo inesperado".[4] Thus he will use "Dios me libre" (God deliver me) with full literal force. Or he will play on one of the words in the phrase so as to give the components a force they do not have taken together alone ("Doy señales de vida con pedazos de muerte / que mastico en la boca, como un hielo sonoro" – I give signs of life with bits of death / which I crunch in my mouth like loud ice). Or he separates through a rhythmic pause elements that commonly go together and thus energizes inert commonplaces ("y un cuchillo / chillando, haciéndose pedazos / de pan" – and a knife / screaming, making its slices / of bread).

Likewise, as Alarcos Llorach points out, Otero often lifts phrases from other poets and, subjecting them to slight joltings and distortions as he grafts them into his own structures, confers on them a new power but at the same time bonds himself in a verbal relationship to the voice he echoes or the image he picks up in his mirror. The procedure is so common with Otero, as a matter of fact, that his poetry gives the impression of a tissue of quotations. Alarcos cites San Juan de la Cruz, Fray Luis de León, Rubén Darío, and César Vallejo. In one poem, "La muerte de Don Quijote" (Don Quixote's Death), we hear the combined voices of Waldo Frank, Heine, Cervantes, Quevedo, Rubén, and Vallejo (Alarcos Llorach, pp. 97-99).

Verbal echoes, however, are easy to pick up. The more cultured the ear, the more it will hear. There are doubtless many more than those mentioned by Alarcos. But more important than the recollection of prefabricated phrases and images for new expressive purposes is the technique that might be called deliberate *pentimento* or palimpsest (I claim no originality for the metaphor), that is, the rewriting of someone else's entire poem, which is thus affirmed, amplified, revised or contradicted, in such a way that the original inspiration or provocation seems intentionally to have been poorly erased from the parch-

---

[4] *La poesía de Blas de Otero* (Salamanca: Ed. Anaya, 1966), p. 90. "At first glance, these are clichés, tags. . . . He uses them to turn them into something new; that is, he breaks them down and brings to life again the sense of their components, thus producing an unexpected expressive effect."

ment and to be constantly legible underneath the new ink. If the achievement of this effect depends in principle on the borrowing technique I have mentioned, it is not always thus dependent and never entirely so. Frequently remarked examples in Otero are the poems of religious anguish – about the God whose transcendence is demanded by the despairing soul but who refuses to answer man's cry – poems which would not be mistaken for the work of Unamuno, but which cast the shadow of his presence behind every word.[5] But the most striking of Otero's palimpsests is "Lo eterno" (The Eternal), plainly an over-writing, to my mind, of Rubén Darío's "Lo fatal" (Fated). The texts of the two poems are reproduced here for the convenience of the reader.[6]

Lo Eterno

Un mundo como un árbol desgajado.
Una generación desarraigada.
Unos hombres sin más destino que
apuntalar las ruinas.

Rompe el mar
en el mar, como un himen inmenso,
mecen los árboles el silencio verde,
las estrellas crepitan, yo las oigo.

Sólo el hombre está solo. Es que se sabe
vivo y mortal. Es que se siente huir
– ese río del tiempo hacia la muerte –.

---

[5] Cf. Joaquín González Muela, "Un hombre de nuestro tiempo: Blas de Otero", *Revista Hispánica Moderna*, XXIX (1963), 137-138: "Nos suena tan pronto a fray Luis como a Quevedo, a San Juan como a Calderón, a Núñez de Arce como a Unamuno. ¡Muy bien! Nosotros no le vamos a criticar eso; a nosotros, que nos agrada creer que la poesía no *sólo* es documento real de un momento histórico, nos complace oír en un hombre tan de 'nuestro tiempo' los ecos de otros hombres de otros tiempos. Pero siempre afinando el oído, para distinguir las voces de los ecos." (He is just as likely to remind us of Luis de León as of Quevedo, of St. John of the Cross as of Calderón, of Núñez de Arce as of Unamuno. Fine! We will not criticize him for that; we like to think that poetry is not only a real document of the historical moment; it gives us pleasure to hear in a man so much of "our time" the echoes of other men of other times. But we must always sharpen our ears to distinguish the voices from the echoes.)

[6] "Lo fatal" is from *Cantos de vida y esperanza*, in Rubén Darío, *Obras poéticas completas*, ed. cit., p. 688. Editions of Darío disagree about the punctuation; I have adopted that of Gerardo Diego in his *Antología*; and I have retained the widely accepted reading "esa [*rather than* esta] ya no siente" in line 2. "Lo eterno" is from Blas de Otero, *Angel fieramente humano* (Madrid; Insula, 1950), pp. 13-14. In this edition as well as in *Hacia la inmensa mayoría* (Buenos Aires: Losada, 1962), the latter part of line 8 reads "Es que sabe" rather than "Es que se sabe." Recently (July 1973) I was able to ask Mr. Otero himself which was the correct reading. Without hesitation he said that the absence of "se" was a printer's error and that the second version, "Es que se sabe," was the correct one. This reading requires synalepha, of course, across the period for a good hendecasyllable. (For numerous suggestions adopted in the translations I am indebted to Professor James E. Irby.)

Es que quiere quedar. Seguir siguiendo,
subir, a contra muerte, hasta lo eterno.
Le da miedo mirar. Cierra los ojos
para dormir el sueño de los vivos.

Pero la muerte, desde dentro, ve.
Pero la muerte, desde dentro, vela.
Pero la muerte, desde dentro, mata.

... El mar – la mar –, como un himen inmenso,
los árboles moviendo el verde aire,
la nieve en llamas do la luz en vilo. ...

(The Eternal

A world like a tree broken off.
A generation uprooted.
Man whose only destiny is
to shore up the ruins.

                    The sea breaks
upon the sea, like an immense hymen,
the trees sway the green silence,
the stars crackle, I hear them.

Man alone is alone. For he knows himself
as a living, mortal being. For he feels himself fleeing
– river of time toward death –.

For he wants to stay. To go on going on,
to go up, against death, even to the eternal.
Looking scares him. He closes his eyes
to sleep the sleep of the living.

But death, from within, sees.
But death, from within, keeps watch.
But death, from within, kills.

... The sea – the sea – like an immense hymen,
the trees stirring the fresh air,
snow flaming in the suspended light. ...)

Lo Fatal

Dichoso el árbol, que es apenas sensitivo,
y más la piedra dura, porque ésa ya no siente,
pues no hay dolor más grande que el dolor
                    de ser vivo,
ni mayor pesadumbre que la vida consciente.

Ser y no saber nada, y ser sin rumbo cierto,
y el temor de haber sido, y un futuro terror . . .
Y el espanto seguro de estar mañana muerto,
y sufrir por la vida, y por la sombra, y por

lo que no conocemos y apenas sospechamos,
y la carne que tienta con sus frescos racimos,
y la tumba que aguarda con sus fúnebres ramos,
¡y no saber adónde vamos
ni de dónde venimos! . . .[7]

('Fated'

How fortunate the tree, that scarcely has any feeling;
more fortunate still the hard stone, because it feels
         nothing at all;
for there is no greater pain than the pain of being alive,
nor greater affliction than conscious life.

To be and to know nothing, and to be without clear
         direction,
and the fear of having been, and a future terror . . .
and the certain horror of being dead tomorrow,
and suffering because of life, because of the dark, because

of what we don't know and can scarcely suspect,
and the flesh that tempts with its tender fruits;
and the tomb that awaits with its funeral wreaths,
and not to know where we are going
nor whence we have come! . . .)

"Lo fatal", a ready-made title phrase that heads the much anthologized poem, is half-transformed into "Lo eterno". The "árbol" (tree), "dichoso" (fortunate) because it is "apenas sensitivo" (scarcely has any feeling), becomes a term of comparison for the world "como un árbol desgajado" (like a tree broken off), and for "una generación" (a generation) – "desarraigada" (uprooted). Then Otero expands the image of the tree along Rubén's original lines : Indifferent to man's solitary anguish, "mecen los árboles el silencio verde" (the trees sway the green silence), or, in the penultimate verse, "los árboles moviendo el verde aire" (the trees stirring the green air). "Pues no hay dolor más grande que el dolor de ser vivo, / ni mayor pesadumbre que la vida consciente" (for there is no greater pain than the pain of being alive, / nor greater affliction than conscious life) is condensed by Otero: "Sólo el hombre está solo. Es que se sabe/vivo y mortal" (Man alone is alone. For he knows himself as a living, mortal being). Otero's entire poem expresses desolate despair, Rubén's expansive treatment of fear – "temor de haber sido, y un futuro terror . . . / Y el espanto seguro de estar mañana muerto" (fear of having been, and a future terror. . . . / And the certain horror of being dead tomorrow) is compressed into "Le da miedo mirar"

(Looking scares him). On the other hand, the brief certainty of "estar mañana muerto" (being dead tomorrow) is expanded : "Pero la muerte, desde dentro, ve. / Pero la muerte, desde dentro, vela. / Pero la muerte, desde dentro, mata." (But death, from within, sees. / But death, from within, keeps watch. / But death, from within, kills.) In a way, Darío's ending "¡y no saber adónde vamos / ni de dónde venimos!" (and not to know where we are going / nor whence we have come!) is Otero's beginning : "Un mundo como un árbol desgajado. / Una generación desarraigada" (A world like a tree broken off. / A generation uprooted).

Besides the verbal and imagistic modes of *pentimento,* we can find here over-painting of a syntactical and a prosodic character. Darío's technique of subjects without predicates, employed with absolute rigor throughout "Lo fatal," is reserved by Otero for only his first and last stanzas. While Otero does not imitate Darío's alexandrine meter, he measures his own hendecasyllables. Witness the care with which the first line of the second stanza is printed so as to constitute the second hemistich of line 4 and to avoid the slightest suggestion of free verse. Indeed, Otero's metrical meticulousness leads him to borrow the rarest trick of Rubén's trade. Lauxar describes it as "rima constituída por voces inacen-tuadas y transformadas en agudas" (rhyme made by placing normally unstressed monosyllables under metrical stress at the line-ending),[7] and cites only four examples, including the one found in "Lo fatal" :

> y sufrir por la vida, y por la sombra, y *por*
> lo que no conocemos y apenas sospechamos,

in which *por* is rhymed with *terror* and by rhyme and syllable count must bear the rhythmic accent of a *terminación aguda,* even though it is an unstressed monosyllable within its syntactic unit. Otero goes Darío one better, trying the same trick but without rhyme to help the stress, in

> Unos hombres sin más destino *que*
> apuntalar las ruinas.

Rhyming *por* with *terror* produces an inescapably comic effect (the kind of thing one might expect in the *género chico*), though *por* at the end of the line does point the way to the prosification, the colloquialization, of poetry. It is this way that Otero follows, giving up the rhyme and forcing the next line to come on without a breath. And from here on, Otero outdoes Darío in poetic trickery : Against the inexorable rhythm of the hendecasyllabic death-march there is the quasi-musical play of sound and word repetition : "Rompe el mar / en el mar." "Un himen inmenso." "Sólo el hombre está solo." "Es que quiere quedar." "Le da miedo mirar." "Seguir siguiendo." The whole stanza on "Pero la muerte. . . ." "El mar – la mar – ." "Un himen inmenso." (One must remark the dark comedy in the opportune shift of gender before the second comparison of the sea with an immense hymen.)

We can imagine how differently Unamuno, with whose tragic sense of life the poem is obviously permeated, would have arranged matters, and in so doing we see how, in another way, the poem is securely within the tradition of the

---

[7] Lauxar [Osvaldo Crispo Acosta], *Rubén Darío y José Enrique Rodó* (Montevideo : Mosca Hermanos, 1945), p. 103.

symbolist technique even though it expresses a realist attitude. The poem consists of some twenty statements : images, thoughts, and sentiments. Their discursive connection with one another, while not difficult to determine, must be largely inferred from their juxtaposition. Yet when we have determined what this connection is, we realize how different "Lo eterno" is from "Lo fatal". "Con Verlaine ambiguo" (ambiguous with Verlaine) is one of Darío's famous phrases. And a much favored symbolist technique for expressing the truth about reality – this, of course, is what Rubén is talking about – is the ambiguous statement that admits of numerous interpretations and guarantees none, so that we have the unexplained symbol, the unrevealed secret, the unanswered question, with the implication that uncertainty itself is the one certain fact. But in "Lo fatal" uncertainty is not the implication, it is the subject, of the poem. It is man's fate to live with the pathos of life's uncertainty.

Quite the opposite is true of "Lo eterno". Let us make the palimpsest more complicated. Otero erases the clear ambiguities of the *mal de siècle*. He cuts off the hope that underlies Jorge Manrique's image of "la mar, que es nuestro morir" (the sea, that is our dying). To Calderón's bidding, "acudamos a lo eterno" (let us attend to the eternal), he replies that this is nothing but an anaesthetic, "el sueño de los vivos" (the sleep – the dream – of the living). He leaves San Juan de la Cruz stuttering "un no sé qué que queda balbuciendo". What is truly eternal is death.

So much for the past and the present of "Lo eterno". Is there no future? If there were no later poems, one might hesitate to say. But the strong this-worldly humanism of Otero's later poems leads one to see hope in the androgynous image of "El mar – la mar – como un himen inmenso", in the regenerative power of nature – an old –and comforting – thought – the tomb, but also the womb that will produce a new, natural man. The snow falls, but it is seen only as it passes through the shafts of natural light.

Princeton University

V

EPILOGUE

Introduction

In the last decade or so, an ever-increasing number of American poet-translators have found in Hispanic verse a previously unsuspected treasure of literary expressiveness. The esthetic and cultural reasons for this profound development are undoubtedly complex, but it apparently is due to the necessity in some American poets to give legitimacy to subjective modes of imagination that were rejected or that remained undeveloped in the dominant strains of Eliotic English-language verse. Chief among the Spanish and Spanish-American poets whose works have been made available in sometimes brilliant and creative translations are Antonio Machado, Juan Ramón Jiménez, Rafael Alberti, Pablo Neruda, César Vallejo, Miguel Hernández, Blas de Otero and other younger writers. In some cases, the act of translating the foreign work becomes almost inseparable from the process of creating original poems since the translated produce achieves an independent existence, fully naturalized in the American idiom.

Whether it be because of themes, new or different rhythms, a distinct type of imagery, or a more subjective vision of life, Hispanic poetry has engaged American writers in unprecedented ways, a trend which is surveyed and evaluated in the following paper by Willis Barnstone – an American poet and active translator in his own right.

The Impact of Poetry in Spanish on Recent American Poetry

WILLIS BARNSTONE

In the last two decades most of the leading poets in recent Spanish poetry have been translated into English – translated largely by American poets. The impact of Spanish poetry on American letters is far more extensive than is generally understood by most readers and critics. Of the twenty best-known poets who have emerged in the United States in the last twenty years, not more than one or two, to my knowledge, has not been engaged at one time or another in translations from Spanish poetry; such a list ranges from Robert Lowell and Richard Wilbur on the one hand to Robert Creeley, Ferlinghetti and Allen Ginsberg on the other.

In the case of all these American poets, the influence is much more real than influences normally charted in comparative literature studies which are based only on a reading acquaintance with an author from another language. For in having themselves translated the poets from Spanish, American poets have been affected in their own poetry by what they have learned and done with the poem in the act of translation. *More important for the American poets than the knowledge of the poem in Spanish has been their own English version of it.* The act of transferring the poem into English immediately gives new possibilities of expression and theme in English, which no mere reading of the original can give. In a word, American poets – who have translated Spanish poetry into English poems, which are valuable in themselves as poems in English – have received the basic impact of poetry in Spanish from their own English versions of the Spanish, and this impact is clearly revealed in their original poetry. They have been affected less by the Spanish than by their own inventions, by what they were forced to do with English words. In effect they were influenced ultimately by themselves, by the new poetic self that came into being as a result of the process of translation from the Spanish.

Before speaking of specific poems and poets, it may be best to review the general orientation of the past few generations of American poetry toward foreign poetry.

In the years immediately before and after World War I, Paris gave poetry in English its avant-garde focus. Our poets went to France. Cummings brought the typographical feats of Apollinaire's *Calligrammes* into American poetics.

Wallace Stevens, Eliot and Pound caught the echo of Laforgue and Corbière in their early work. France had had its hand on the pulse of European poetry for more than a century, and American writers, with other Europeans, came to learn from Mallarmé, Valéry and Baudelaire what ironically these French poets thought they had learned from the American Poe. Even into the thirties, Hart Crane discovered Rimbaud, and Marianne Moore roamed through centuries of French verse, bringing the fabled animals of La Fontaine modernly into her own bestiary.

When the French introduced *surrealism* into European poetry – the last major school of poetry they opened to world letters – the Americans (as well as the English) were not listening. We were to learn a form of surrealism, not in the mid-twenties, like the rest of Europe, but thirty years later in the mid-fifties; and not from the French but from Spaniards and Spanish Americans, from Vallejo and Neruda, Lorca, Hernández and Aleixandre, who handled elements of surrealism with far greater mastery than had their French innovators.

After World War II, American poets awoke to the poetry of Spain and Latin America. The awakening came late, but with great magnitude and alertness. This discovery of poetry in Spanish has been followed by the most recent encounter with Russian poetry – Marina Tvetaeva, Voznesensky, Mandelstam. Today the poetry of the Soviet Union and Spain and Latin America has completely replaced France as the primary outside force acting upon American verse.

As early as 1946, Angel Flores presented Neruda to the American reader through his New Directions bilingual edition of *Residencia en la tierra*. García Lorca was introduced through the translations of Stephen Spender and Rolfe Humphries. Then after 1959 three English language volumes of the poetry of Antonio Machado were published, and poets like Octavio Paz, Guillén, Jiménez, Alberti, Vallejo and Hernández suddenly appeared in English translation in virtually every American literary periodical which claimed any attention to world literature. By this we mean the *Hudson Review, Partisan Review, Literary Review, The Sixties, The Nation, Poetry*, etc. Lorca, because of the nature of his tragic death, was the first poet known in this country. Now he is only one of the many.

As it became known to American poetry, Spanish poetry not only brought to our attention the work of major foreign poets; it also profoundly influenced the course of American poetry. These American poets who have been so affected by the work of Spanish and Spanish-American authors represent, as was said, virtually all American poets whose important work became known in the fifties and sixties : Lowell, Wilbur, Ginsberg, Denise Levertov, W. S. Merwin, Robert Bly, Thomas Merton, Alan Dugan, Robert Blackburn, Robert Creeley, Stanley Moss, Ferlinghetti, Mark Strand, James Wright. In his most recent collection of poems, *Near the Ocean*, Robert Lowell even goes back to Quevedo and Góngora, from whom he includes four sonnets in his own English version. Allen Ginsberg found an ally in the *ismos* of Huidobro and Parra. The sly profundity of Borges, the cosmic passion of Guillén and Aleixandre, the politics, color and virile exuberance of poets like Hernández, Blas de Otero, Paz and Neruda found immediate counterparts in American poets who rendered them into English.

Mark Strand and Muriel Ruykeyser translated books of Octavio Paz. In April, 1968, Jorge Luis Borges read his own poetry in Spanish at the Poetry Center in New York and his work was read in turn in English translation by Strand and Dugan.

How did it happen that American poetry became at one moment receptive to Hispanic influence? What was the nature of the change in American poetry which made the impact of Spanish verse possible? To answer this, we should first say a word about American poetry in the early fifties.

As we know, following the great radical work of Eliot, Pound, Crane, Cummings, Stevens and William Carlos Williams, American poetry settled into more sedate patterns of form and content. It settled into the university, with all its organized intelligence and tenuous reality. The fire in experimentation, in the discovery of modernity, diminished. American poetry was constricted to what in an unjust oversimplification has been called *academic or square verse.* And indeed even in its physical appearance, the upright rectangle of eight or ten classically riming quatrains appeared to dominate the pages of our quarterlies, just as the excellent New Critics, who had spawned the mild-tempered fish, were dominating criticism. The picture is abundantly clear if one glances at a typical anthology of the time – John Ciardi's *Mid Century American Poetry,* Twayne, 1950, which reflects the poetry of the period. Then, without warning, in violent exasperation and rebellion, new movements came upon the scene : the Beats and the Black Mountain School, the Projectivists. At this point one may ask what had Spanish poetry to do with these internal American movements. Again the answer is not expected. Spanish poetry acted as a *mediating* force in American poetry. It provided the one area of taste in which beat, square and inbetween could meet. *Replacing French influence,* it expanded the horizon of American poetry, making it again more of the world, less of the classroom.

The recent New Directions book *Poems and Antipoems,* 1967, by Nicanor Parra, containing translations by Merwin, the late W. C. Williams, Thomas Merton and Ginsberg, well illustrates the role of Spanish poetry as a mediating force. If one knew only the work of these poets from the mid-fifties, it would seem almost impossible that a decade later they would be joining forces to translate a Chilean poet. The change, however, is not simply one of tolerance on neutral grounds. It is rather because their own poetry, in part through the impact of Spanish verse, in part through becoming more of our century and less of a particular American school, has moved closer together.

Miguel Hernández is an example of one Spanish poet who has profoundly affected recent American verse. His poetry has been known for some time, examples appearing in the *Chelsea Review, Chicago Review,* the Bantam anthology *Modern European Poetry,* and most recently in the last issue of the *Sixties,* one of the most topical and influential magazines in American poetry, whose issue number 9 is dedicated to Hernández, containing six articles and a selection of his poems in Spanish and English translation. Again we may ask what did American poets find in Hernández. They found passion and imaginative freedom. Hernández possessed all those qualities which American academic verse, at its worst, seemed to lack : dramatic force, a surreal and irrational substratum of feeling and imagery, a blatant powerful sexuality, an elemental and universal passion expressed in nature images not restricted to the city or the American scene.

In speaking of poets who have emerged in the fifties and sixties, M. L. Rosenthal in *The New Poets* writes, ". . . it has occupied itself salutarily with translation – this is particularly true of Bly, the most active 'theorist' of the group, who has tried valiantly to propagandize for the poetry of Lorca and Neruda, among other European and Latin-American poets. From Lorca especially [*The Poet in New York*], the group has learned to value the surrealist image highly". Rosenthal further speaks about the poets' "interest in translation as a clue to effective use of imagery" as well as the possibility of a new "social poetry" as embodied in Neruda's writing.

We may remember at this time that the English poets of the thirties – Stephen Spender, Louis MacNeice, Laurie Lee, W. H. Auden – all went to Spain and were also affected by the clear image and the social poem. We see this in Auden's poem "Spain, 1936", MacNeice's *Autumn Journal,* or in any number of those poems by Spender – "Port Bou," "To a Spanish Poet" – where in perhaps his very best poems he is imitating Lorca or Altolaguirre. The impression, nevertheless, upon English poets and upon American novelists, Dos Passos and Hemingway, was principally Spain itself, its people and its terrible Civil War, and only secondarily its literature. The American poets of today, in translating the poets of both Spain and Latin America, have found not only social but poetic allies in Spanish lands.

Examples are many. We may consider the work of James Wright, one of the finest poets of our generation, who has translated Machado, Hernández, Lorca, Jiménez and Vallejo. The hallmarks of Spanish verse are obvious in his poem "Eisenhower's Visit to Franco, 1959", which he prefaces with a line from Unamuno, "we die of cold, and not darkness", or in his poem "In memory of a Spanish poet" for Miguel Hernández, where he speaks of Hernández's death in the prison hospital.

> I see you strangling
> Under the black ripples of whitewashed walls.
> Your hands turn yellow in the ruins of the sun.
> I dream of your slow voice, flying,
> Planting the dark waters of the spirit
> With lutes and seeds.

More important, however, than the obvious examples which contain Spanish subject matter are other poems in which the lessons from poetry in Spanish, and from his own translations of it, have been absorbed into his own creations. Such a poem is "Spring Images". Those who are familiar with Wright's work would not find the precedent of this poem in either his earlier book, *Saint Judas,* or in work written by other poets in America. The semi-surreal nature images come from Spanish, and my own guess is from Lorca's "La canción de la muerta pequeña".

Spring Images

Two athletes
Are dancing in the cathedral
Of the Wind.

A butterfly lights on the branch
Of your green voice.

Small antelopes
Fall asleep in the ashes
Of the moon.

We may also mention that at least one other new element in recent American poetry has an Hispanic origin. This is the *concept of the brief poem*. Except for the epigrams of a Ben Jonson or a Blake, the history of poetry in English notably lacks any strong tradition of the brief poem. In the last decade, however, poets such as Merwin, Creeley, Levertov, Wright and Bly have discovered the force of the brief, highly visual lyric. It is no accident, surely, that these poets are among those who have been most directly involved with poetry in Spanish. The recent anthology of short poems, *The Sea and the Honeycomb*, edited by Bly, published by the Sixties Press, contained more poems translated from Spanish than from all other languages. Interestingly, after Spanish the greatest number of short poems were translated from Arabic – the Arabic of Moslem Spain. Of course, the *hai ku* has also been imitated by American poets, but usually the poets affected have not turned to writing short poems in English but simply the specific form of the *hai ku*. The Iberian tradition, with the Arabic *qasida*, the *jarchas* of Spanish Jews and Moors, and the brief lyrics of the *cancioneros*, the short verses of Lope, Lorca, Jiménez and Machado, has provided American poets with a rich source of striking lyrics in their most concentrated form.

Finally, we may say that poetry in Spanish, and especially the poetry written in the mid-thirties by Hernández, Lorca, Neruda and Vallejo, has been a source of liberation for American poetry. Suddenly, the night became blacker and more sexually vibrant, the day became hotter and the sun burned across nature with a new metaphysical passion. The polite wit and elegance of dominating academic verse gave way to a fundamental preoccupation with man's intense inner world, and this solitude lost in a cosmic environment. The poets of the Spanish language have been a focal point in our return to a much greater moment in American poetry : in which man is again humanely and intimately aware of the many levels of his terrible solitude, of the dream element in the unconscious – expressed through appropriate imagery – and the outer world, with its things and anti-things, its violence, its political bureaucracies, its lovers, its black night and its sun.

Indiana University

SPANISH WRITERS
of 1936

*Crisis and Commitment in the Poetry of
the Thirties and Forties*

AN ANTHOLOGY OF LITERARY STUDIES AND ESSAYS

———

*Edited by Jaime Ferrán
and Daniel P. Testa*

TAMESIS BOOKS LIMITED
LONDON